Dutchtown

Dutchtown

A City Centre Design b

OMA/Rem Koolhaas

Michelle Provoost, Bernard Colenbrander, Floris Alkemade

NAi Publishers

Contents

Architecture

MARKERMEER

OOST-VAARDERS-PLASSEN

Gem. Almere

Wilgenbos

Lepelaar-plassen

Noorder-plassen

BUITENVAART

RING N702

Almere-Buiten

PAMPUSHAVEN

OOSTVAARDERSDIJK

MARKER KANT

ALMERE-STAD

RAND STAD

ALMERE-STAD

ALMERE

Almere Pampus (toek.)

MOZIEK WIJK

Kon. Beatrix Park

HOLLANDSE KANT

Weerwater

N703

IJMEER

Almere poort (toek.)

GOOISE KANT

Wetering Park

Waterlandse Bossen

Almere-Hout

De Steiger

DE STEIGER

Marinastrand

MARINA-WEG

A6

Kromsloot park

Almere-Haven

Waterlandse Tuinen

N27

Gem. Kathedralen-bos

Almere

Zilver-strand

GOOIMEER

GOOIMEERDIJK-WEST

IJSSELMEER

GOOIMEER

Gem. Naarden

BESTEVAER

Gem. Huizen

Huizen

A27

Introduction

Urbanization in the Netherlands knows no limits. There are of course still places where at first glance the city seems far away, but here too the urbanite's ways are slowly pushing the traditional rural customs in the direction of folklore. Since the city is getting bigger and bigger and changing in appearance and composition, there is a constant stream of work for Dutch urban planning, in an institutional context that advances new directives and themes every now and again. The urban planning culture fostered by the government still resonates with the notion of the 'compact city', which implies containing urban growth as concisely as possible within designated areas and imposing sharp restrictions elsewhere. The reality outside shows us the effects of that policy, but also something else: a highly dispersed pattern of low-density housing and industrial development, advancing deeply into areas we considered 'rural' up to now. Evidently, the fragmenting influence of the Randstad is inescapable. Urbanization and decentralization are taking place in the Netherlands. A knock-on effect of this thinning out of the substance of the city are signs of a certain romanticism in the old urban centres. Existing cityscapes are conserved in their perfection thanks to the restrictive policy of the authorities, as has happened in the centre of Amsterdam. In other centres the coveted historical ambience is stage-managed, fabricated with completely new development if necessary, as with the curious kitsch of the De Resident complex in The Hague.

In the historical city the relation between the centre and outlying districts is by definition one between old and new. Occasionally, things are the other way around: the chronology of urban development does not advance with distance from the core. This is true of Almere for instance. The first pieces of this new town in the polder, located on the edge of the Randstad, rose up a quarter of a century ago. It was built on the polder expanse and lacked not only a context but also a historical core. Some years ago it was decided to fulfil the constantly postponed dream of a genuine town centre with the realization of a design by the Office for Metropolitan Architecture (OMA) headed by Rem Koolhaas. The assignment was right up his street. Ever since Delirious New York in the late 1970s, Koolhaas had exhibited more than a fleeting interest in artificially fabricated urban identity, an interest that has now found its way onto construction sites in controversial projects such as Euralille. In the meantime, the design of Almere's new centre has developed to the point where various architects are engaged in the detailed elaboration of plan components; those invited include Alsop & Störmer, de Architekten Cie. (Frits van Dongen), Claus en Kaan, and Kazuyo Sejima (with Greiner and Van Goor Architecten).

The operation in Almere is an interesting case for various reasons, and thus also the occasion for this book, published to coincide with an exhibition at the

Netherlands Architecture Institute (NAI). Firstly, the issue of the identity of the city centre is one of the most important cultural tasks at the moment, certainly in view of the direction that seems to have been adopted in Amsterdam and The Hague. Owing to the absence of historical context in Almere, the degree of difficulty of the task is revealed to the full: the centre of Almere is of necessity an entirely synthetic cultural invention. Secondly, the project is of importance as the urban expression of the Polder Model. The plan bears the signature of OMA but also tangibly expresses the confrontation with other parties – the local council and the developers approached (MAB and Blauwhoed Eurowoningen), each with its own priorities. The discussions among the parties provoked an extraordinary concentration on what the substance of the programme of today's modern city could be. In what way can a public domain be shaped? Does it amount to the sum of all private territories together, or does a recognizably public zone for everybody leave its imprint?

Finally, the new Almere is also of note as an element in the oeuvre of OMA, which is now of a genuinely staggering thematic richness. The NAI hopes to keep track of the development of the office in the coming years.

Kristin Feireiss, director

Michelle Provoost / Bernard Colenbrander

Dutchtown

The dilemmas of the polder town

The newest settlement in the recently created Flevo Polder still had no name. IJdrechtstad, Zuidweststad, Almere...? Even its precise location was still undecided: a mere grey spot, it drifted aimlessly across the feature-less map of the polder. A nameless, placeless town: these conditions give some idea of the incredible freedom enjoyed by the town's planners. The polder was a perfect tabula rasa, without context, without history, without obstacles, and with a topography that would be shaped entirely in accor-dance with their wishes. Since there was nothing, everything was possible. It sounds like the secret dream of every modernist town planner but in fact the generation of planners who went to work in Almere was rather discomfited by the total lack of restrictions. They no longer took their cue from the optimistic and intrepid modernists, but from the deferential prac-tice of urban renewal, with its small-scale development, assimilation and consultation.

Almere, an experiment both radical and dated, was developed under the most paradoxical circumstances imaginable. It repudiated modernism, but had to live with the modernist legacy in the planning institutions. It was modern because it set out to be new and different; postmodern because it has sought to link itself to the past. Though based on small-scale develop-ment it was supposed to become a city for hundreds of thousands of people. It is the outcome of an urban design plan drawn up by architects behaving as sociologists.

Almere was the product of an allergy. With a projected population of between 100,000 and 200,000 inhabitants, it was similar in size to the Bijlmer urban expansion near Amsterdam (120,000) and the new town of Zoetermeer near The Hague (300,000), both of which were exponents of a self-assured, modernist urbanism, with towers in the park and separate traffic circuits (Bijlmer) and a clear hierarchy of neighbourhoods and districts (Zoetermeer). They were based on an established urbanist tradition dating back to the Second World War and were designed by teams of specialists who knew exactly what was expected of them. In the Netherlands, as indeed all over the Western world, the results of their labours had come under increasing criticism. The large, luxurious tower blocks in park-like surroundings were accused of causing high-rise depression, massification, loneliness and alien-ation. The concept of space embodied by the Bijlmer was interpreted as emptiness. As it happened, the high point of this sociologically inspired criti-cism coincided with the completion of the Bijlmer and the beginning of the planning for Almere. The new town's historical task was clear: Almere would be the very antithesis of the modernist model; above all, it would be different from the Bijlmer.

Thus were the main themes laid down that have continued to dictate the development of Almere and its architecture up to the present day. Almere is inextricably bound up with the debate about fullness versus emptiness; about small town urbanity versus the anonymity of the metropolis; about social idealism versus the affluent society; about allergy as inspiration and architecture as amenity; about the creation of identity and about the creation of a centre. Almere is an architectural theme park in which all the themes can be traced back to the 1960s.

The city as environment

1971

Almere's planners did not have to start from scratch in developing a new urban model. Aldo van Eyck's 'story of another idea', written in 1959, already incorporated the sociological critique of post-war housing production in its emphasis on the importance of the encounter, the in-between, the small-scale and the familiar. What Van Eyck meant by this became clear in the urban renewal plan he helped draw up for the Nieuwmarkt neighbourhood in Amsterdam (1971, concurrently with the planning of Almere). Like a Dutch Jane Jacobs he pointed out the importance of neighbourhood communities and the need to preserve social relationships when carrying out urban renewal work. He believed it was possible to design the encounter and visu-alize the personal.

In the nineteenth-century Rotterdam neighbourhood Oude Westen, small-scale urban renewal was carried out on a grand scale. The scheme was a radi-cal departure from the prevailing modernist urbanism, both in layout and in the organization of the development process. Conventionally draughted plans were discarded, to be replace by an agenda, policy, slogans, community meetings and drawings with text balloons.[1] The full-fledged urban life the planners discovered in the inner-urban neighbourhoods had to be facilitated and visualized, the architecture had to be the counterform of its occupants. According to the new paradigm, the built environment could not be separated from the life that took place in it. Indeed, it had a profound effect on the resi-dents' happiness and chances of self-fulfilment. The city was an environment capable of offering its inhabitants visual stimulus but equally capable – through the absence of stimuli, as in the monotonous modernist city – of making their lives hell. It was up to urban designers to provide enough visual 'arousal' to prevent city dwellers from falling into a state of passivity, even apathy. This 'Rotterdam approach' subsequently spread to urban renewal schemes in the Dapper and Kinker neighbourhoods in Amsterdam and Schilderswijk in The Hague.

It also spread, through the architecture, writings and above all the teaching of Aldo van Eyck, whose work was an embodiment of this view, to the plan-ning establishment. From 1970, Van Eyck's many disciples started to infiltrate the institutes and government planning agencies from whence they helped disseminate a bureaucratic version of this 'other idea' about the relationship between humanity and environment. So it was that the Rijksdienst voor de IJsselmeerpolders (IJsselmeerpolders Development Authority, RIJP) which was responsible for the development of Almere, presented a curious mixture of planning establishment figures and young urban designers inspired by the lessons of sociology and psychology.

It was a typically Dutch mixture, if we are to believe to the American histo-rian James Kennedy. In Nieuw Babylon in aanbouw, Nederland in de jaren zestig (Building New Babylon, the Netherlands in the Sixties)[2] he argues that one of the distinguishing features of Dutch culture in the turbulent 1960s was its readiness to assimilate alternative and experimental tendencies which he attributes to a fear of being thought old fashioned. Politicians, university governors, lecturers and other 'regents' all deemed it wiser to move with the times rather than try to no resist developments that could not in any case be halted. This was especially evident in the 1960s when, compared with France or the United States, say, the rowdy demands for democratization were relatively smoothly accommodated by way of institutional reform. With remarkably little resistance or violence, the generation of '68 managed to bring about change and to win a place for itself among the rulers rather than continuing to face them across the barricades. This applied especially to the universities in the liberal (some might say anarchic) city of Amsterdam, but even at Delft University of Technology the formal hierarchy between lecturers and students in the faculty of architecture evaporated completely. The new was automatically accommodated within the status quo. This trend continued with even greater force into the 1970s.

This mechanism of assimilation accounts for part of Almere's ambiguity. It accounts for the curious combination of experiment and bureaucracy which saw a big bureaucratic body like the RIJP joining forces with progressive young designers to design 'the city of the future'. Almere has continued to pursue the trend set in the 1970s with architecturally adventurous neighbourhoods in the 1980s, and in the 1990s with its daring choice of OMA. 'Repressive tolerance' was the term coined by the left-wing intelligentsia in the 1970s for this practice of disarming the potentially subversive by absorbing it. Is this what is happening now to Rem Koolhaas, himself a member of the generation of '68, and his provocative plan for a new city centre for Almere?

2 The Bijlmer,
   Amsterdam South-East.

3 Masterplan for Almere as
   polynuclear town, IJsselmeerpolders Development Authority
   1978.

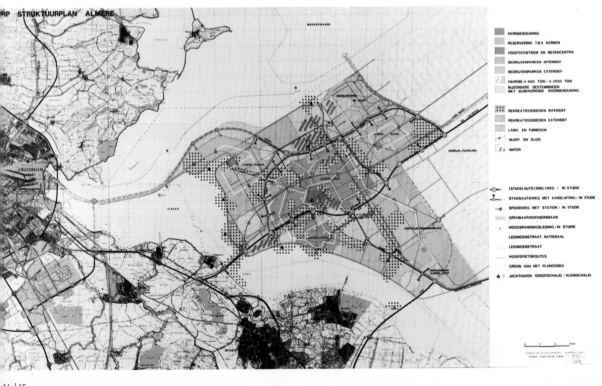

New Town of the affluent society

The IJsselmeerpolders Development Authority (RIJP) is a worthy government agency with a history dating back to 1919. Until 1984, the RIJP was solely responsible for the planning of the three IJsselmeerpolders: North and South Flevoland and Markerwaard, the last of which never eventuated. The authority planned everything, from the draining of the land to the layout of the villages and the design of (model) farms.

In 1959 the RIJP contracted out the planning of the capital of the polders, Lelystad, to the country's most celebrated town planner, Cornelis van Eesteren, known for his 1930 General Extension Plan for Amsterdam. By the time it was Almere's turn to be planned, however, Dutch society had changed so much that Van Eesteren's staunchly modernist vision had become an anachronism. The RIJP decided that rather than getting someone else to design the last Dutch New Town, it would do the job itself, to which end it put together a special project office from among its own ranks.

In retrospect, the spatial planning debate of those years sounds disconcertingly similar to the one that has dominated the 1990s. That earlier discussion, which is summarized in Petra Brouwer's Van stad naar stedelijkheid ('From city to city life),[3] revolved around fullness versus emptiness and suburb versus metropolis. Then as now the concept of the Randstad as a rim of self-contained cities around a large and (relatively) empty 'green heart' was under threat from the expansive activities of towns in the central area. Using the autonomy granted them, these municipalities were able to build to their heart's content, thereby frustrating a national planning policy that had been in place since the late 1950s. The truth was that urban life was no longer defined by city boundaries but by high mobility, consumption and individualism. 'The city' no longer corresponded to its form but to a way of life. To the horror of the planning fraternity, the Dutch had discovered suburban living.

There was no question of Almere surrendering to this new urbanity and abandoning the traditional urban model. On the contrary, the planning of Almere was conceived as an offensive against suburbanization. Yet it was also an attempt to exorcise the disadvantages of the big city. In short, Almere was the outcome of a dual allergy, to the suburb and to the metropolis, and as such it represented the triumph of the provincial town.

For the basic layout, the RIJP had opted in 1969 for the polynuclear city, a city composed of a number of cores separated from one another by green belts; a city, moreover, consisting entirely of low-rise development. In choosing the polynuclear layout, a concept that can be traced back directly to Ebenezer Howard's garden city idea, the RIJP was translating national planning policy to the scale of a city. Since 1966, when the Second Report on Spatial Planning appeared, that national policy had been dictated by the defensive strategy of clustered dispersal (an oxymoron in that it amounted to 'concentrated deconcentration'). Faced with the two frightening extremes of megalopolis and uncontrolled suburban sprawl the government had elected to steer a middle course of controlled expansion in a few, carefully selected 'growth centres'.

Almere was no post-war reconstruction New Town after the style of
Hoogvliet and Alexanderpolder near Rotterdam, or Buitenveldert and
Amsterdam North near Amsterdam, where urban development followed a
strict, Russian-doll sequence of house, neighbourhood, district, city, that was
intended to provide city dwellers with a sense of security and structure.
Almere was a New Town of the affluent society whose denizens wanted freedom of choice and diversity; it was a New Town for the discriminating
consumer. Each of Almere's cores was to be given a distinct identity which
was reflected in the choice of name: Almere-Haven (harbour), Almere-Hout
(forest), Almere-Buiten (country) and Almere-Stad (city). They would be
homogeneous urban quarters tailored to different social groups and in this
respect they can be seen as the forerunners of the lifestyle-planning of the
1980s and 1990s. The cores were interspersed with extensive recreational
green zones, located close to the houses and eminently accessible. All the
necessary amenities would be in place before the arrival of the first residents. In short, Almere was a little paradise that would entice even the
staunchest Amsterdammers to the polder.

It was a paradise marked by fear of the big city: the socially homogeneous
neighbourhoods had none of the drawbacks of the old, dilapidated low-
income neighbourhoods where immigrants made up a growing percentage of
the population; the division into smaller units was intended to foster the kind
of community spirit that was only to be found nowadays in villages and small
towns; and while the themed neighbourhoods may have looked suspiciously
like sprawling suburbs Almere's designers had no sympathy for suburban
anonymity. What they sought was a form that possessed a clear centre and a
sense of community, a form that offered people with a suburban lifestyle the
decor of an old-fashioned town.

Social interaction and unclotting

In 1971, the RIJP commissioned the architect Frans van Klingeren to draw up
what was in effect a manifesto for the future of Almere. Van Klingeren's
unusual career had seen him develop from a builder of sheds to a designer of
'social capacitors', multi-function buildings in which the various uses and
users encroached upon one another's space to a barely tolerable degree. The
clearest illustration of this technique is the Meerpaal in Dronten, in the
northern part of the Flevo Polder. The Meerpaal (1967) is a roof with glass
walls, 'a 50 by 70 metre lot, covered over and heated' in Van Klingeren's own
words.[4] It is minimal architecture enclosing maximal activity: the interior
contains a market, theatre, library, restaurant and a sports field, all of which
are intended to be used concurrently. Van Klingeren regarded any inconven-
ience arising from such use as positive: the building was a didactic space
where involuntary encounters with other people and activities would serve
to stimulate people, widen their horizons and promote self-development. The
Meerpaal was the purest expression of Van Klingeren's obsession with social
interaction.[5] He was convinced that the post-war emphasis on the home
rather than the living environment had resulted in increased social isolation.
The solution was 'unclotting': unravelling the mono-functional clots and
reconnecting the functions in such a way as to produce a maximum of social
interaction.

1971

translation:

pebble stones:

changing concepts of family
commune
changes of partner

shorter working hours
floating working hours
men and women working part-time
changing attitudes towards work

mankind is the master of free will
the mobile individual is a man of choice
incompleteness is an essential characteristic
the mobility of workers and citizens

enable more by doing less
the campus versus Eindhoven
the house and the car

the responsibility of the designers

play versus sport

what is needed is not technology but a different way of thinking
disposable objects or disposable people
mankind's purpose is to be on the move
the second renaissance

enriching landscape = improving openness
offices become   office landscapes
schools become   learning landscapes
shops become   consumer landscapes
factories become   industrial parks
houses become   residential landscapes

public:private   1:1 $1^1/_2:^1/_2$ instead of 1:2 (Aerdenhout)

openness as an evolution of democracy
unclotting versus privatization

culture for the few is on the decline
culture is of itself not an aim
éducation permanente

scarcity as a fiction
habitable roadways rather than inhabitable cities
the built structure as a means of communication
Bosch and Breughel

Plato
behind the appearances lie innate ideas.

Attenberg:

Sah der Kenner ein Kieselsteinchen mit einem Schneeklümpchen behaftet
den Tannenwaldabhang herunterrieseln. "Eine Lawine" schrie er und
stürzte fort. "Wo?" fragte der ahnungslose Spaziergänger, aber man
könnte ihm nicht mehr antworten, er war bereits begraben.

kiezelsteentjes: wijzigende gezinsopvattingen
                  commune
                  partner veranderingen

                  verkorting arbeidstijd
                  de floating werktijd
                  half man / half vrouw werkend
                  de veranderende werkhouding

                  de mens is de heer der keuze
                  de mobiele mens is een kiezende mens
                  het onvoltooide is een wezenskenmerk
                  de mobiliteit van werknemers en burgers

                  doe meer met minder
                  de campus versus Eindhoven
                  het huis en de auto

                  de verantwoordelijkheid van de ontwerpers

                  spel versus sport

                  nodig is niet de techniek maar een ander denkraam
                  wegwerpdingen of wegwerpmensen
                  het doel van de mens is onderweg zijn
                  de tweede renaissance

                  verlandschappelijking = openbaarheid
                  kantoren worden   bureaulandschappen
                  scholen worden   leerlandschappen
                  winkels worden   kooplandschappen
                  fabrieken worden   industrieparken
                  huizen worden   leeflandschappen

                  openbaar : privé   1:1 1½:½ i.p.v. 1:2 (Aerdenhout)

                  openheid als evolutie der democratie
                  ontklontering versus privatisering

                  cultuur voor enkelen gaat ten onder
                  cultuur geen zelfstandig doel
                  éducation permanente

                  de schaarste als fictie

                  bewoonbare wegen boven onbewoonbare steden

                  het bouwwerk als communicatiemiddel

                  Bosch en Breughel.

Plato

achter de verschijnselen schuilen aangeboren ideeën.

The social interaction sought by Van Klingeren was implicit in his slogan 'enable more by doing less': a certain degree of imperfection in the living environment encourages residents to get involved, whereas a perfectly laid out neighbourhood leads to passivity. Needless to say, Van Klingeren had an unshakable belief in spatial determinism, the notion that human beings are profoundly affected by their physical surroundings. It follows that architects have the power to influence people's behaviour and to add to their enjoyment of life. Although frequently associated with the Forum group, Van Klingeren's work differed from theirs on one essential point. Forum members adhered to the (unwritten) rule 'enable more by doing more' with the result that their favourite buildings reflected a horror vacui that only theoretically invited participation. Instead of the inhibiting fullness of Forum architecture, Van Klingeren opted for a stimulating emptiness as form and a programme of mixed uses.

The future Van Klingeren envisaged for Almere was based on these ideas. His desire to design the ideal city for the creative, playful individual – for homo ludens – reflects the influence of Constant's New Babylon. Shorter working hours, it was reasoned, meant more leisure time and because the work was less arduous people would have more energy left over for self-realization. Everything pointed to the need for more social interaction at the expense of the isolation of the private dwelling. Social interaction allows for a more positive attitude to the notion of the 'masses' than modernism ever permitted, with scope for interaction between mass and individual. In this new

6

De magische doos van Van Klingeren

DRONTENS· NIEUWE GEMEENSCHAPSCENT[...]

bibliotheek
Nederlands Architectuurinstit[...]

Parool 7·11·67

EXTRA

Morgen opening
door koningin

„Dit gemeenschapscentrum hier in Dronten heeft 3.2 miljoen gulden gekost. Als je me nou m'n gang liet gaan, maakte ik iets voor nòg minder. Ik zou best een budget willen hebben van 2½ miljoen."

De Amsterdamse architect Frank van Klingeren (48) zegt dit temidden van het bedrijvig geraas van allerlei mannen, die de vele „laatste werkzaamheden" verrichten aan het gemeenschapscentrum De Meerpaal in Dronten, Oostelijk Flevoland.
In de hoek van de enorme rechthoekige ruimte, in een prachtig gebetoncilinder. (officiële

ARCHITECT FRANK VAN KLINGEREN in De Meerpaal te Dronten (en op het Eidofoorscherm)   foto BERT SPRENK[...]

DOOR
PIET VAN DEN ENDE

(Concretisering in Dronten: Er is maar één afgesloten vergaderzaal. Alle overige ruimten zijn in open verbinding met de grote ruimte. Terwijl men in het ronde theater naar een toneelstuk kijkt is het mogelijk dat men op de achtergrond het ge[...] [...]hoort, het ge[...]

activiteiten is gebleken, dat men heel goed wat achtergrondgeruis kan verdragen. Je hebt hier natuurlijk niet de stilte uit het Concertgebouw als Mengelberg op de lessenaar heeft getikt, maar vergeet u niet, een halve eeuw geleden was die stilte in de [...] ook niks. Toen had je [...]

horen er helemaal bij. Ik we[...] veel met Van Soest."
En terug naar het onderwerp storingsfactor is zeer positi[...] man, die niet naar het theate[...] komt er toch mee in contact [...] misschien de volgende keer o[...] werkt bevruchtend."

world the landscape acts as a metaphor for social interaction: stores become shopping landscapes, offices work landscapes, houses domestic landscapes, and schools learning landscapes. Van Klingeren imagined Almere as a coherent landscape for living and playing.

6 The Meerpaal, Frans van Klingeren, Dronten, 1967.

7 Het Parool, 7 November 1967.

8 HP, 18 May 1974.

Leftish fellows

Almere had a direct link with the Amsterdam urban renewal operation in that the latter would have been impossible without the relocation prospects offered by Almere. The principle of 'building for the neighbourhood' applied in Almere, too, even though they were building brand-new neighbourhoods for as yet unknown residents. The planning and the architectural elaboration of Almere-Haven were all about facilitating Van Eyck's 'encounters' through the creation of squares, courts and likely meeting places. The architecture did its best to avoid giving residents an impression of monotony and massiveness by providing them with a wealth of small-scale variation. It has to be said that Van Klingeren's slogan 'enable more by doing less' had not really caught on here; in fact this was the most detailed decor ever designed for a housing project in the Netherlands. Long before the phenomenon of Disneyfication had been identified, Almere was busy fulfilling its promise. The architecture in the centre of Almere-Haven was postmodern, referring with its mini-canals and canal houses to the time-honoured streetscape of Amsterdam.

-18-5 1974   43

loog Scheek, projectleider Frieling, ontwerper Koolhaas „...voortdurend onder druk..."

eelt die twijfel met wijlen prof. Stei-   de mensen erg fragmentarisch bezig.   le pap willen hebben. Met die werkgelegen-
a. Steigenga   destijds: „Er   zitten   „Sjef S^h^^' ^^n van de socio^^^^ houdt   heid daaraan gekoppeld, dat is voor m^^

Almere aimed to be 'an ordinary little Dutch town' with the security and conviviality found in the historic neighbourhoods of the capital.

9 Themed neighbourhoods in Almere-Haven, 1972.

10 Urban design study for Almere-Haven by H. van Willigen, 1971.

The RIJP's Projectbureau Almere consisted of a small group of people, half of whom were young academics without any practical experience. Dirk Frieling was project manager, Teun Koolhaas urban designer and Sjef Scheek worked in the team as sociologist. They described themselves as 'leftish fellows'.[6] Yet they were neither so left-wing – nor so academic – as some of their Marxist contemporaries at Delft University of Technology and the Sorbonne in Paris that they were prepared to foreswear working under the pernicious capitalist system altogether and retreat to their studies. They preferred to work within the system so as to be able to put their socially-minded ideas into practice. As it happened, their ideas were perfectly in tune with the policies of the centre-left cabinet led by Labour Party leader Joop den Uyl which took office in 1973. One of its stated aims was to put 70 % of housing within the reach of low and minimum incomes.

The trickiest question facing the designers of course was how to design a city from scratch in the absence of the usual mechanisms of growth and development. How does one go about organizing chance? How does one prepare for the future when there is no past on which to base one's predictions? The answer was: not by drawing a blueprint but by treating the design as a process. They produced a basic plan along the lines of the one made 25 years earlier for the post-war reconstruction of Rotterdam, but while they showed the infrastructure and land uses, they omitted the orthogonal structure of the Rotterdam plan. So unsure and critical were they about their own profession that they did no more indicate the various development zones with circles on the map; the rest they left to the architects.
The first residential area of 500 dwellings shows the evolution of a new urbanist cartography. Orthogonal development made way for a Barbapappa-style development consisting of groups of houses arranged in a series of circular clusters. These 'beads' were then strung together on a green ground to form a necklace of mini-neighbourhoods. Each bead-cluster stood for a different lifestyle of the individualistic conurbation-dweller: 'traditional', 'extravert', 'experimental core housing', 'indoor emphasis on the communal', 'indoor emphasis on the individual'. Higher up the planning scale, at the level

9

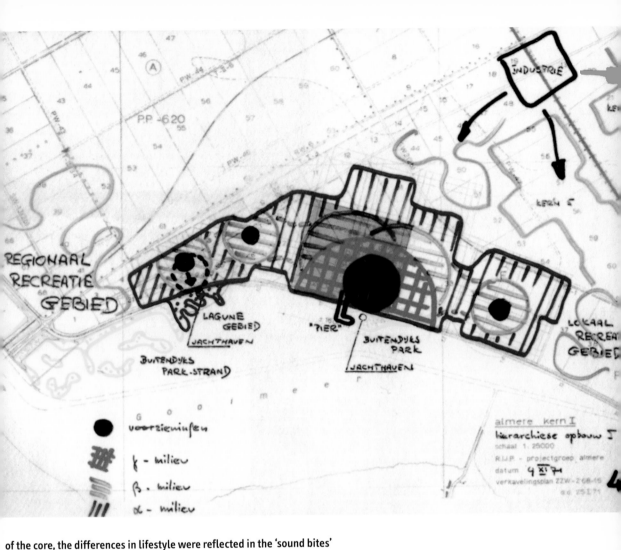

of the core, the differences in lifestyle were reflected in the 'sound bites' tacked on to Almere: Haven, Stad, Buiten, and so on. This emphasis on different types of residents and the moulding of the design around difference and individuality rather than the collectivity of the reconstruction period, gave rise to a curious counterpart to the social welfare state. The 'lifestyle' neighbourhoods were conceived of as positive ghettos where the shared way of life would guarantee mutual contacts and social interaction.

Three architects, Dick Apon, Joop van Stigt and A. Mastenbroek, were commissioned to design the houses in the first section of Almere-Haven; they were also required to design an appropriate environment now that these were no longer seen as two separate tasks. Urbanism was played out, architecture took over its task. Along the canals in the centre of Almere-Haven, Dick Apon designed brick canal houses with stylized gables. Street elevations were divided up into small-scale units; tower blocks and large urban blocks were taboo. The houses displayed considerable variety in floor plan and dwelling type. Density was highest in this central zone where buildings ran to three or four storeys, diminishing progressively as one moved away from the centre. In the residential areas, low terraced houses executed in brick with timber accents fronted onto 'home zones', roads that prioritized pedestrians and cyclists while restricting vehicles to little more than walking pace. Not that cars could have speeded in any case, for there were no straight stretches of road longer than 50 metres. A greater contrast with the Bijlmer could not have been imagined. A dedicated bus lane circled around the various Courts, Counties, Commons and Willow Groves and there was a separate ring road for motor traffic. Wherever one lived, greenways, recreation parks and marinas were never far away; the informality of the camping ground, so often held up as a model during planning, was closely approximated.

If the bureaucratic and modernist traditions of the RIJP found concrete expression in the separate traffic routes and the isolation of the housing function, they were even more apparent in the organization of the design process. The latter duly came under fire from the 'leftist' media because it failed to comply with the new democratic norms of local discussion and participation introduced a few years earlier in the context of urban renewal.[7] Projectbureau Almere was accused of a lack of openness: it worked behind closed doors, in the ivory towers of the RIJP. Even though there were no actual residents to consult as yet, surely a survey of domestic requirements could have been carried out among the target groups? The design had been made for the people but not by the people, so the complaint went. As a result, Almere ended up being compared with its sworn enemy, the Bijlmer; Almere, too, was a technocratic and authoritarian design, only in low-rise. On essential points it resembled that which it opposed. Once again, ran the criticism, it was a case of middle-class designers imposing their ideal notions on ordinary people. The only difference from the Bijlmer planning was that the RIJP included the slogan of 'humane planning' in its technocratic banner.

The contemporary critique can be summed up as follows: the plan for Almere may seem modern and benevolent in its social ambitions but in the end these are empty slogans and the plan itself is old-fashioned because it is based on an anti-urban model and 'back-to-nature' nostalgia.

Some of these charges undoubtedly had a basis of truth and can be explained by the dichotomy in the planning process noted earlier: a younger generation of designers with progressive ideas working within the margins dictated by an established coordinating authority. The fact that Almere-Haven is neither one thing nor the other probably explains why as early as the late 1970s the entire professional community turned against what Almere represented in terms of planning and architecture – 'the new insipidity' as Carel Weeber dubbed it in an ironic echo of New Objectivity. By the same token, the fact that the design was tackled pragmatically rather than radically is probably the reason for the enormous public success of Almere which, in its short existence, has simply kept on growing in both size and popularity.

POLITIE

1982

Almere-Haven was a form of simulated urban renewal, something of a fairytale time–space cocktail the ingredients for which had been prepared by the

Forum culture and which accorded perfectly with the intensely nostalgic bourgeois taste of the time.

It was in these surroundings that OMA built its first project on Dutch soil: in 1982 Rem Koolhaas designed a police station on the outskirts of Almere-Haven. It was an inspired piece of casting: cheek by jowl with 1970s replicas of Amsterdam canal houses exuding safety and familiarity, Koolhaas was asked to conjure up a vision of law and order. Once again, allergy proved to be a fruitful source of inspiration: Koolhaas's design displays an unmistakable aversion to the paternalistic conviviality of Almere. Though unpretentious, the police station is also uncompromising, consisting chiefly of a single wall with letters – and this in the context of Almere-Haven where there had been an explicit ban on straight lines and boxy shapes. It is first and foremost a graphic design in which the desolation and emptiness of the polder is reconstructed in the emptiness between the letters P O L I T I E (Police). In the battle between the comforts of fullness and the freedom of emptiness OMA had made its position perfectly clear.

Nowadays, given the advances neo-modernism has made in the meantime, it is difficult to credit just how new and different OMA's police station was in the early 1980s. It was succeeded by a series of events that were to earn Almere an international reputation as the place where architectural creativity could be indulged to the full. They resulted in a fairly imposing collection of discrete architectural moments, set against a backdrop of decorous, perhaps slightly dull, neo-modernist buildings. The largest and

11 Almere-Haven.

12 Police station Almere-Haven, OMA, 1982-1986.

most important of these architectural moments – De Fantasie (The Fantasy) – is Almere's contribution to the rejuvenation of the Dutch housing culture. In retrospect, this competition for 'unusual homes' launched in Almere in 1982, can be regarded as the unofficial and unintentional start of the campaign for informal urbanism and liberalization of the housing market that came to dominate urbanism in the 1990s. In 1984, on a secluded grassy lot with only the most basic infrastructure, there appeared as part of a small collection of individualistic creativity two self-build houses. One was by Jan Benthem and Mels Crouwel, the other by Dick Bruijne and Peter Loerakker. Both were variations on conventional construction technology (the first high tech, the second low tech) and on conventional domestic programming. The Benthem Crouwel house lacked the structural mass normally associated with a sense of psychological and physical well-being. It offered total transparency of the living space coupled with a caravan-like solution for the requisite amenities. Loerakker and Bruijne's house was based on the idea of a LAT (living apart together) relationship so that part of the programme was executed in duplicate, resulting in two juxtaposed cubes.

De Fantasie touched a chord with a sizeable group of potential home buyers/builders. These well-educated, relatively affluent urbanites who were looking for self-realization via their living environment did not find it easy to build and live as they wished in the Netherlands. Here was an untapped market and Almere was alert enough to seize the opportunity.

De Fantasie was duly followed in 1986 by the aptly entitled De Realiteit (The Reality) for in this and the various other housing expos held in Almere from the late 1980s onwards, experimental construction was completely subsumed in an efficient sales machinery, complete with estate agents, brochures, model homes and the like. The Music, Film and Rainbow districts offered, within the finely tuned marketing formulas of the construction industry, a barely acceptable level of variation. In nearly every instance these were one-family homes. Here and there a kitchen had been linked in ingenious fashion to the living room or a void or a striking bay window had been added, but the main emphasis was on form and colour. Some of the projects looked back to the great social housing tradition of the past, for example by paraphrasing the 1927 Stuttgart Weissenhofsiedlung (a row of houses by Kees Rijnboutt), while others practised 'modern acropolism' (villas on an artificial hill by Sjoerd Soeters) or offered buyers a poor man's version of a Hollywood villa (semi-detached houses by Erick van Egeraat).

In most cases the design theme amounted to little more than a certain aimless cheerfulness which, compared with what is produced in the average expansion area, was at most a little more flamboyant. The fact remained, however, that confirmed conservatives from the Amsterdam canal zone found it all mightily tempting and were moved to sigh: 'I'd buy one of these houses tomorrow, if only they were somewhere else'.[8]

These architectural manifestations, in which the accent was on creativity, individuality and originality, gave a neo-modern twist to the emphasis on brick-framed lifestyles with which the planning of Almere had begun. The individuality of the occupants was now rendered in the architecture as well. The concern for diversity of form and differences in lifestyle which found architectural expression in the home during the 1980s was a direct product of the notions of individuality and identity conceived during the era of urban renewal and Forum. As such, the 1980s did not represent a break so much as a change of course, reinforced by the growing influence of the market. The social ideals on which Almere had been founded made way for a collection of designed objects predicated on city marketing. Having started out as a social experiment Almere has become more and more a middle-class paradise so that today the city is synonymous with bourgeois taste in the Netherlands.

Almere followed in the footsteps of urban renewal where, from the early 1980s, the focus of attempts to improve the social environment was on 'architectural quality', streetscape and 'cultural value'. For Almere, where the architects and variation in architecture had played a bigger than normal role right from the beginning in Almere-Haven, this was nothing new. From variety in brick, the architectural production shifted to neo-modernist variety, led by OMA's police station. Almere became one big, open-air architectural expo featuring a succession of attractions: De Fantasie (1982), De Realiteit (1986), Music District (1990), Film District (1992), Rainbow District (1995), Personal Housing (1999) and City Centre OMA (2005).

13 De Realiteit (housing expo), 1986.

14 Weerwater lake showing site of future centre with Cees Dam's town hall in background.

Almere-Stad

In terms of form, Almere-Stad, which followed in 1979, was a good deal
more robust than Almere-Haven and in the centre in particular it even
bordered on the 'objectivity' of a grid structure. 'Rationalistic' models had
become markedly more popular in the architectural world since the late
1970s. Almere's own centre plan was inspired by the plan of Barcelona, a
work of art that was well on its way to becoming an icon of post-modern
urbanism.[9]

But Almere continued to be less a case of urbanism than of architecture,
an interesting sum of individual buildings. That architecture was from the
very beginning readily accommodated within a neutral spatial framework.
In Almere almost anything was possible. Just as the surrounding polder
landscape was a perfect tabula rasa for the construction of the city as a
whole, so the city plan provided a flexible context for the principal buildings. Ironically, this also applied to the most important building in terms
of civic authority: the town hall. The choice of Cees Dam, who had also
designed a new city hall for Amsterdam, was a sign both of Almere's
dependence on the mother city Amsterdam and of its approaching autonomy: in 1988 Almere became a city in its own right. The Almere town hall is
Cees Dam's masterpiece and the only monumental structure in Almere-
Stad erected according to the rules of the grid. The building, expensively
fitted out from top to bottom, could easily have been interpreted as a
monumental diktat if, that is, there had been an empathic context. But that
is lacking in Almere. To the extent that buildings communicate here, it is
not with one another but far beyond the city boundaries: the architecture
that is springing up in Almere is – on this spot at least – self-evidently new
and autonomous.

In the same classical mode as the central grid was the composition devised
for the first residential areas of this new core, which consisted of massive
blocks with articulated corners, an axial arrangement of main streets and
visual axes culminating in square-like spaces. The grid was an attempt to
transpose the tried and tested urbanity of Barcelona and Berlage to Almere-
Stad and in so doing to rid the town of its provincial character. It did not
succeed, however. The strict segregation of different types of traffic resulting in wide bus lanes plus endless cycleways plus separate motor vehicle
routes together with the popularity of the attached single-family home
effectively sabotaged that ambition.[10] Over the years accessibility by car and
the concomitant demand for parking space came to occupy an increasingly
central place in the planning task. This task was further affected by the
consequences of the spread of private home ownership.

Almere remained problematic, not least because the immediate encapsula-
tion of the impetus of De Fantasie removed the sting from an emerging
cultural tendency towards informal, not to say anarchic spatial behaviour,
which might well have produced something stunning in the ambivalent
Almere context.

In July 1999, however, the newspapers carried reports of a housing scheme
being planned for Almere's third core, Almere-Buiten. Though the 500
houses involved would be realized in collaboration with construction
firms and housing associations, future residents would nonetheless enjoy
considerable freedom of choice along the lines of the controversial Wilde

Wonen (a Dutch version of the consumer-led, anything-goes type of development found in the US and other countries but previously taboo in the well-regulated Dutch housing market). The formula appears to be a mixture of the adventure of De Fantasie and the institutional and commercial efficiency of the older themed neighbourhoods. And thanks to OMA's plan for the centre of Almere-Stad, it looks as if Almere's collective presence may finally be about to extricate itself from the embrace of the well-meaning but now played-out historical archetypes of Barcelona and Berlage.

15 Almere Town Hall, Cees Dam, 1979-1986.

New centre, new history

The consistency displayed by the planners of Almere is quite remarkable for the Netherlands. Although the architectural expression and even the spatial layout have followed the fashions of the day, the basic principles of Almere have remained intact for two decades. The polynuclear city still exists, as does the idea that one of the nuclei should be the 'capital'. In the 1990s this found expression in the city council's decision to take a step foreshadowed back in 1971: to build a civic centre for all Almere, on the shore of Weerwater lake in Almere-Stad. Though the planners of 1971 had no clear picture of what the future centre would look like, they had a clear idea of what it should contain: key urban facilities such as the largest retail concentration, hotels, library, exhibition space, cinema, Youth Advisory Centre, and so on. It was to be the hierarchical and geographical hub of the dispersed structure of Almere.

The commencement of this enormous enterprise, which will take many years and involve many millions of guilders, is a sign that Almere's steadily growing self-awareness has almost come of age. For a long time Almere was a mere appendage of Amsterdam; an immature outpost of the conurbation, dependent on Amsterdam for employment and with a population drawn from Amsterdam. The image of Almere was that of a dull dormitory town possessing no entertainment of its own. Recreation in green surroundings is not in itself enough to satisfy the modern urbanite's metropolitan requirements; the homo ludens of the 1990s looks for amusement in fun shopping, the cinema or night life rather than indulging in endless creativity in specially designed 'play landscapes'. To accommodate those aspirations and to be able to grow to 180,000 and thereafter to 250,000 inhabitants, Almere needs a centre – to satisfy present needs and to lure future residents.

That centre is being explicitly presented as a place of concentration and centrality. In other words, the authorities have opted for a traditional concept of the city centre as the geographic and programmatic heart of the city. There were alternative visions: in 1996, both MVRDV and Neutelings Riedijk produced (competition) proposals in which the projected growth in housing (20,000-30,000 dwellings by 2013) was accommodated not in the existing urban areas but along the traffic artery connecting Almere with the old land, the A6 between Amsterdam and Lelystad. The A6 runs through the middle of the various cores that make up the polynuclear structure of Almere and as such can be viewed as a central axis. MVRDV's conclusion was clear: instead of being treated as a negative barrier, the A6 should be regarded as a centre; not as a trajectory from A to B, but as a boulevard lined by houses and offices. This urban boulevard would link Almere with Schiphol Airport, the Amsterdam Woods, the North Sea, etcetera, while the A6 would stimulate development in the northern sector of the Randstad.

With its concept of a centre linked to the traffic infrastructure, MVRDV was simply applying to Almere contemporary theories about the utilization of motorways for urban development. But of course this notion of Almere as Edge City was completely incompatible with the plans for a lakeside city centre. Almere had opted for the traditional position of the city centre as a point in space, not a line; a central, densely built location that would elevate Almere to 'a real city'. Rather than develop its eccentric character any further, Almere had chosen to crown its evolution from provincial town to full-fledged city with a compact city centre.

Almere continues to work with all the vigour of a young, self-made city not only on its future, but also on its past. A city without any history, it has set about creating one for itself. The oldest building until recently was a grain silo dating from the 1960s, but with the erection of an old lighthouse, a gift from the Ministry of Waterways and Public Works, Almere has now acquired a monument from the 1950s.

Almere aspires to be a 'complete city'. With the same energy it applied to securing a licence for a World Trade Center (1998) it has now embarked upon the construction of a medieval castle that is intended to make good the lack of a romantic wedding venue. It is composed of elements from a medieval Walloon castle mounted on a sturdy concrete understructure. The licence for the WTC meanwhile puts Almere on a par with 350 cities from Abu Dhabi to Zurich and from Tokyo to New York, not to mention the mother city of Amsterdam.[11]

Both these actions were initiated by the alderman who was also responsible for the city centre, C.W.J. van Bemmel. It is therefore logical to surmise that

ll three projects are the products of the same philosophy: Almere as self-
made city. Almere aspires to be complete and proceeds to provide itself with
everything it still lacks or has never had: historic monuments, world trade
and a convivial city centre.

Plans

In Almere-Stad a large tract of undeveloped land awaits the arrival of the
centre. Its contours on one side are inscribed by Cees Dam's town hall. To
north and west of the site shopping streets wait to be connected up to one
another. Weerwater lake on the remaining side has the potential to become a
genuine waterfront. The only discordant note in this setting was struck by
two of the oldest blocks in Almere-Stad, public housing used to rehouse 'anti-
social' elements from the Amsterdam urban renewal areas during the 1980s
and which was no longer entirely appropriate to the prestigious image
Almere had in mind for its city centre. The blocks were accordingly demol-
ished, the residents disappeared, and Almere in effect underwent its first
urban renewal operation. Left-wing compassion for the lowest incomes and
the 1970s philosophy of 'live to play' made way for 1990s social democracy
with its calculating citizens and officials and the slogan: 'Almere is living,
working, shopping'.

In 1990 the Almere city council engaged an external project manager for the
next step in the city's development. Though the municipal departments
responsible for the successive construction of Almere-Haven, Almere-Stad,
Almere-Buiten and Almere-Hout formed a well-oiled machine, their routine,
based as it was on the patterns of the residential neighbourhood, was not
automatically suited to the development of a city centre. Project manager Kor
Buitendijk was requested as an 'outsider' to concretize the council's unspo-
ken wishes regarding the centre. Buitendijk was an old hand, having been
present at the birth of urban renewal through his work in Rotterdam's Oude
Westen, the neighbourhood which, as already noted, served as the testing

16 Impression of Almeres
medieval castle.

17 The A6 as the centre of Almere,
MVRDV, 1996.

18 Floris Alkemade.

19 Kor Buitendijk.

Floris Alkemade

The process of extrapolation

ground for urban renewal in the Netherlands. Thereafter he had worked on various restructuring projects in several historical town centres. It seems reasonable to assume that his ideas about what constitutes a city have been formed by his experiences. These experiences encompass ideas about small-scale development, differentiation, conviviality, identity, and visual arousal dating from the 1970s; they also include an acquaintance with the participation of market operators during the 1980s and the development of various PPP constructions (Public Private Partnerships). The achievements of both periods were reflected in the memorandum of basic principles and later on in the discussions about OMA's design.

Buitendijk concluded that Almere was not a city, but an aggregation of houses. In order to change this he identified all the parameters required to make a 'city': a mix of uses and high density; shops, hotels, bars and public transport as well as dwellings; 'negative' aspects (red light district, junkies, etc.) along with the positive. It is as if the very neutrality of Almere whetted Buitendijk's faith in urbanity (warts and all) as a means of escape from the town's mediocrity and provincial character.

Analysis

The City
No one visiting Almere can fail to admire the resolute way the fastest growing city in the Netherlands has managed to coordinate its turbulent growth and – despite its somewhat negative image – is unobtrusively on its way to becoming the country's fifth largest city. Almere is made up of extensive residential districts. Yet the patterns on the city map reveal no visible consolidation indicative of a city centre.

The houses in these districts are new, spacious and readily available. Almere has the image of a city inhabited solely by happy young families. In our office the town is sometimes compared with the mating grounds to which some animal species withdraw in order to reproduce.

The typologies of these housing areas, which would normally only be found as extensions to an older core, stand here in splendid isolation, separated from one another by vast green belts.

Almere presents the picture of a city that was in fact never meant to be a big city. The original plan, designed at a time when cities and city life were suspect, was based on five equal cores, each with its own centre and local government offices.

Despite this intention, the continued growth of the city has generated so much mass that a natural but unplanned pressure has been put on the heart of the most central core: Almere-Stad.

With a little good will, the development of Almere can be compared to the birth of a star in which a cloud of

gaseous matter attains so much mass at a certain moment that the collective gravity causes the core to implode.

What this metaphor means in terms of Almere-Stad is that its centre is subject to ever-increasing pressure for new and bigger programmes capable of satisfying demands for strong, specifically urban functions. Those demands consequently shaped the brief for the city centre design competition organized by Almere city council. Four practices were asked to produce a plan for a truly 'urban' centre.

The centre

Just as the enormous expanse of the polder has been consistently shut out and rendered invisible by housing or stands of trees, so the positioning of the centre of Almere would appear to have been inspired by a certain fear of direct confrontation with the vastness of the surrounding space.

Rather than confronting the boundless waters of the IJsselmeer, the centre sits cosily beside the Weerwater, an artificial lake created in the polder.

What strikes one immediately about the centre is the huge amount of empty space. This is partly due to the far-sightedness of the local authorities who deliberately left large areas of the centre undeveloped. Now, twenty years later, these areas can be filled with the

ike Riek Bakker in Rotterdam, Buitendijk bent local politicians to his will. Rotterdam made the leap southwards across the river to the languishing industrial area of Kop van Zuid, Almere made the leap to City. Buitendijk presented the council with a vision of the kind of city they should aspire to become, told them how they could achieve this and set up a project office accomplish the task.

Almere has to wrest itself from its image as a mere dormitory town for Amsterdam. The town must be rescued from what Richard Ingersoll described in Casabella as a psychological dilemma: 'Almere is caught in the spiritual contradiction of belonging to the sprawl of the Randstad more than to its own geographical place.'[12] Almere must now become a place in its own right, a 'complete city' with more businesses and employment, more inhabitants, more attractions and more infrastructure. The present centre of Almere-Stad comprises one or two shopping streets with branches of all the well-known retail chains and a Market Square with a few pavement cafés. It is the sort of centre one might expect to find in a small provincial town but which certainly does not reflect the metropolitan lifestyle of its residents and still less the ambitions of its council. The town must consequently make a 'qualitative leap', or as OMA has put it, a 'quantum leap'.

The run-up to this leap was the Nota Centrum Almere 2005. Nota van uitgangspunten (Almere Centre 2005. Memorandum of principles), published in January 1994 and largely the work of Kor Buitendijk. A little while later a multiple commission (a Dutch variation on the invited competition) was awarded to four Dutch architectural practices. Gert Urhahn, bureau Quadrat, Teun Koolhaas and OMA were asked to translate the urban design vision contained in the memorandum into a design for the new city centre.
The memorandum provided concrete guidelines for the programme and concept for its spatial configuration. The programme called for double the present amount of retail space in a compact shopping precinct, more bars and restaurants with something for everyone, cultural buildings such as a

22 Almere city centre with
   Weerwater lake in the middle,
   Almere-Haven below and
   Almere-Stad immediately
   above.

23 The Almere grid (1978) after
   modification by Ashok Balothra.

23

classic urban centre functions that Almere has not been able to afford until now.
Another reason for the large areas of empty space is the dedicated bus lane that cuts a wide swathe through the centre. The present rather lean complement of shopping streets is unable to bridge these physical and psychological barriers effectively and so give the centre a sense of cohesion.
Because these same shopping streets have been developed in the most archetypal form they present a dispiriting picture of the Dutch building culture of the past twenty years.
The original plan for the centre was modelled on the orthogonal grid of the Barcelona street plan. The centre as built, however, lacks the essential qualities of its model, namely equivalency of streets and freedom of movement in two directions.

The centre is encircled by a ring road but owing to a dogmatic traffic philosophy that has prioritized cycle and bus traffic, every form of continuous car traffic through the centre itself has been systematically blocked.
This cumbersome and somewhat frustrating strategy applies only to car traffic. With its dedicated bus lanes and cycle paths the city is ideally laid out for public transport and cycle traffic.

theatre, library and museum, and a separate business centre next to the railway station. Nor did Almere overlook the residential element, for there is a correlation between a city centre and population growth. To lure new residents an attractive city with an equally attractive centre is necessary; conversely, an ambitious centre needs the patronage of an affluent population. The housing programme, with its more expensive owner-occupied houses, was therefore aimed at wealthier, older residents.

The spatial interpretation of this programme put forward in the memorandum reveals a continuation of blocks in grid formation, an underground bus lane, and a cultural 'street' with cinema, museum and library and terminating in a theatre jutting out into the waters of Weerwater lake.

In addition to the programme, the memorandum also contained a number of key indicators as to the type of city centre the city authorities had in mind. In the first place, they saw the centre's accessibility as a major trump card vis à vis surrounding towns and cities. No historical city has anything to touch Almere's modern car traffic system. The council saw this as its greatest competitive strength with the result that solutions for car traffic, public transport and parking occupied a prominent place in their thinking. The memorandum also suggested moving the dedicated bus lane that traverses the centre underground.

In the second place, the council wanted a distinctive centre, something special, something different: 'An "overall theme" will distinguish Almere from other centres. This is necessary because of the lack of picturesque, historical buildings and because the branches of the national retail chains are gradually turning Dutch city centres into look-alike clones'.[13] In a variation on Van Klingeren's 'Let all Zuidweststad be an agora!', the cry was now: 'The centre as heterogeneous social space!'.[14] Almere wants an attractive townscape with a skyline that will give the flat and spread out city a focal point and a recognizable silhouette. The new centre must furnish Almere with a postcard image, a unique logo that will distinguish it from all other cities.

24 A first sketch: looking for an element with a different logic and scale within the amorphous sea of houses.

Basic premises

This analysis of the existing city centre gave rise to a number of basic premises that influenced the development of the design.

• to develop an urban identity, the centre needs a much greater density and a much greater diversity of programme;

• the motor car must be given a fully integrated place in the centre; the Calvinist notion that everything to do with the automobile is by definition bad, is a poor basis for the development of an urban centre;

• without compromising the obvious advantages of the dedicated bus lane, the latter must nonetheless be prevented from fragmenting the city with its long empty stretches of barely crossable carriageway;

• because the street pattern in the centre does not function as a grid, the plan should not attempt to conform to the pseudo-grid but investigate new possibilities;

• the retail programme is subject to so many set formulas in the Netherlands that shopping centres are getting to look more and more alike. The shopping precinct in Almere must therefore have a distinct identity of its own that is not determined primarily by the shops themselves;

• in the midst of such an abundance of low-rise, small-scale residential development, the city centre must introduce a larger scale of buildings and uses;

• the position of the centre must be visible and palpable throughout the city.

The four practices each received a box with information material, photo albums and maps, together with a photograph of the lamentably flat skyline of Almere as incentive. They also received intensive guidance from the city of Almere. They were able to tap into the considerable knowledge and experience accumulated by the municipal services where a whole range of specialists stood ready to advise them. The contribution of the market operators was of particular interest since implementation of the centre plan would necessarily involve some from of Public Private Partnership. Having gathered all the information they needed, the four practices spent a further month considering their separate designs.

Teun Koolhaas kept to the grid; hardly surprising, since he had been one of its designers in the 1980s. He improved the accessibility of the centre by creating a direct link with the A6. Gert Urhahn accommodated the retail programme in a canal-lined kasbah with underground car park. OMA designed a megastructure with three separate levels for traffic, shops and houses. The design produced by the Rotterdam-based bureau Quadrat was the favourite of almost the entire jury.[15] The lakeside location of the cultural buildings promised to give Almere a distinctive waterfront with the museum and theatre visible from the A6; at the same time their composition of city blocks in grid formation fitted in well with the existing layout and with Almere's relatively low skyline.

It was precisely this rather unadventurous accommodation that Kor Buitendijk objected to: this conservative plan did not result in anything radically different from what already existed. If Almere's 'quality leap' was to succeed it had to be made visible in the new city centre. It therefore stood to reason that the centre should not be modest but sensational; not low but high; not spread out across the grid but concentrated. There was only one plan that satisfied these criteria and it was the one by OMA. It was indeed based on 'a different idea' and in one fell swoop it conferred a metropolitan status on the skyline and image of Almere. It seemed that only the most famous Dutch architect was capable of altering the visual identity and image of Almere in the same way as Frank Gehry had done for Bilbao. ⋯⟩ 45

25 First studies of the possibility of concentrating the programme in two areas, near the station and beside the lake

26-28 First concept models investigating the carré as a large-scale concentration of programme.

29 1 Weerwater
2 Carré
3 Town Hall
4 Station
5 Office strip
6 Rape seed strip

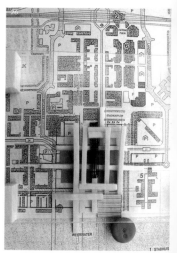

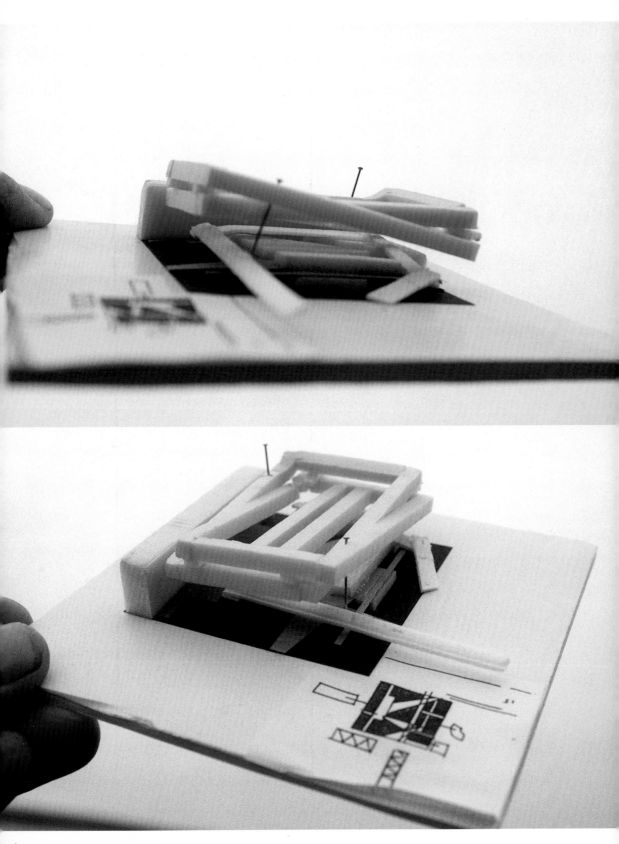

Initial studies

Identity

The first sketch models investigated whether it was feasible to compress the council's programme, which was intended to fill all the remaining open spaces, into two key areas: one beside Weerwater lake, the other behind the railway embankment and directly connected to the station.

This radical concentration was used as a means of forcing an urban identity. We felt that compressing many different programmes in this way might precipitate a chain reaction of interaction, both in the spatial image and in the way the centre functions.

By systematically superimposing different programme elements we ended up with a layered city centre. The studies resulted in a division into three 275 m by 275 m levels: the lowest level for cars, the middle one for shops and other public programmes and the top level for dwellings.

After intensive lobbying by Buitendijk and after a personal presentation of the plan by OMA's project architect, Floris Alkemade, the other jury members began to see something in OMA's shock treatment and on 1 December 1994 the plan was officially declared to be the winner. Nonetheless, the plan remained controversial, the main criticisms being that it was too abstract and that it did not link up with the existing centre. These matters would need to be resolved cooperatively during the planning process.

30 Early study for the manipulation of the ground plane at the carré location.

31 Existing traffic structure: centre can only be reached via a circuitous route.

32 Proposal for extra motorway link-up across the lake and an extra exit from the ring road north of the railway station.

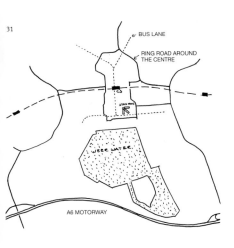

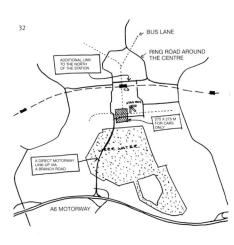

Traffic

In addition to designing a level devoted exclusively to car traffic, we made two suggestions for improving the centre's accessibility. The first was for a direct motorway link-up via a branch road running across Weerwater on a floating bridge or else along the western shore of the lake. The second was for an additional link to the ring road immediately to the north of the station.

The Weerwater-motorway link-up would save motorists having to drive halfway round the ring road to reach the centre. The link to the north of the station would simplify traffic circulation through the centre and also improve the accessibility of the office strip we had planned for this spot.

During meetings prior to the actual competition presentation, city officials remained stubbornly attached to the existing traffic structure. Both modifications of the access system were categorically rejected because the additional volume of traffic involved would put some parts of the existing centre under intolerable strain while making others redundant.

Megastructure

1994

OMA's competition design was made by Rem Koolhaas, Floris Alkemade and Juliette Bekkering. They decided on a radical approach that introduced a completely different scale into Almere: a megastructure that concentrated all the required uses in separate layers on top of the infrastructure.

Of all the sites allocated for the new centre development, OMA used only half. As in post-war Rotterdam, whose pioneering spirit and enormous energy Almere shares, a large area was left empty as reserve space for unforeseeable later developments. In treating emptiness as a spatial promise for the future OMA made clear which side it was on in the architectural debate about emptiness versus fullness that had been going on since Almere's birth. OMA was for the promise of the future, for optimism and for the confidence implied in leaving space undeveloped. OMA and Rem Koolhaas obviously had their roots in the 1960s, but with Van Klingeren rather than with Forum.

OMA deliberately played concentration and emptiness off against one another: by consolidating the business programme around the station, space was left for a park to the north of the station; by consolidating the retail programme, the 'rape seed strip' east of the planning area could be left undeveloped and the boulevard freed for a cultural programme.

The required programme was concentrated in two locations: a business centre of 200,000 m² behind the station and the civic-commercial centre on the barren tract of land between the town hall and the lake. In both locations OMA abandoned the grid structure with its horizontal separation of infrastructure and development, opting instead for a vertical zoning with the different uses stacked one above the other.

The business centre stands on a deck that inclines gently over a partially sunken bus lane. Below the deck is a two-level car park, above it sixteen office towers rising to a maximum height of 80 metres. Acting as intermediary between these two extremes is the entrance level, where a shopping floor below the towers will feature 'more or less office-related shops'. The ····} 50

33 Further elaboration of the housing level with more perforations.

Elaboration

In one of the conceptual models the first version of the curved ground plane was introduced, with a result that the half-buried volumes of the car parks (in rigid blue foam) disappeared under a gently rising ground surface.

This strategy allowed us to develop a gently rising and falling pedestrian domain in the centre that in one smooth movement spans the bus lane and the connecting road. The layer beneath the rising ground plane is the exclusive domain of car, bus, cycle and goods traffic.

In order to give equal weight to both the motorized and pedestrian worlds, the retail programme can be reached from both the lower and the ground level. A third layer – a two-storey slab containing the housing programme – was placed over the entire surface of the retail layer.

Multiple perforations in the different layers ensure an adequate incidence of daylight throughout and allow the layers to be connected at various points. Our intention from the outset was to make the separation between the different layers as diffuse as possible and to connect them to one another wherever possible.

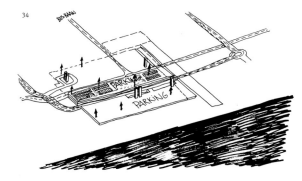

34

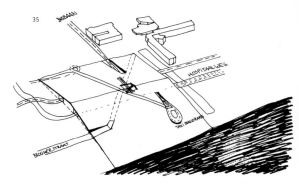

35

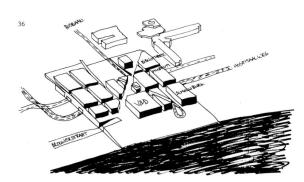

36

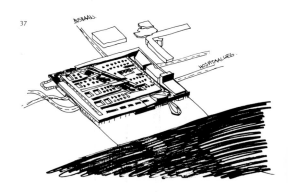

37

34 The roadstructure continues on the parking level.

35 The curved ground plane between the town hall and the lake with roads running underneath.

36 The curved ground plane is punctuated with blocks of shops that are still arranged orthogonally at this stage and bisected by the diagonal axis.

37 The layout of the housing level with streets; a diagonal slash mimicking the diagonal shopping axis below becomes a garden on this level.

38-40 Side view of carré perspective with the different layers placed one above the other.

41 The bottom, car park level, and on the same level the road and parallel to it the bus lane which forms a T-junction here.

42 Sliding the car park volumes under a raised ground plane results in the curved ground plane.

43 Later versions investigate how other programmes might be accommodated below the raked ground plane.

44 First layout for the third level containing the housing programme.

45 Further elaboration of the housing level with more perforations.

46 The housing level consisting of patio dwellings fronting onto ordinary but raised streets, accessible to car traffic.

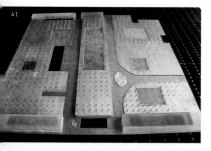

41

42

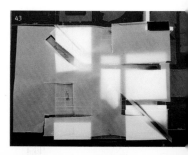

43

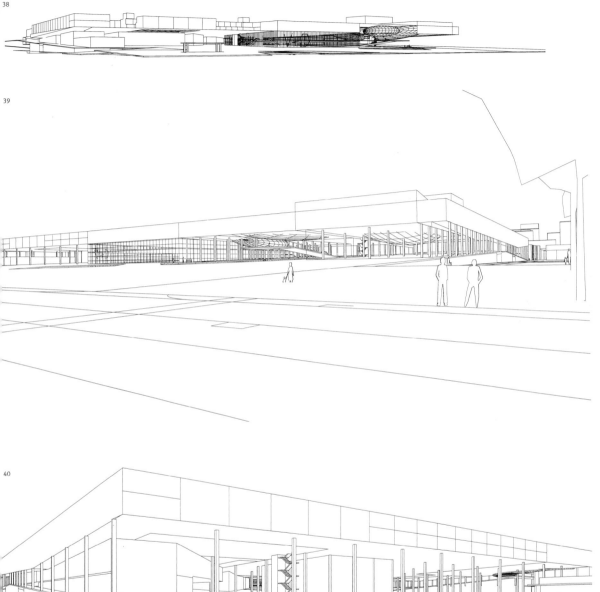

38

39

40

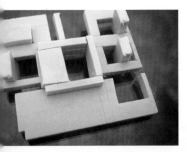

45

46

towers are connected to one another by overhead walkways. In what appears to be a reconfiguration of OMA's 1978 competition design for the Hague city hall, with its staggered succession of office slabs, low-pitched Almere acquires an instant skyline.

The scheme OMA presented for the centre zone is based on a doubling of the ground plane: a curved deck that resolves the barriers of Hospitaalweg and the bus lane by simply folding itself over them. Expensive underground infrastructural solutions are thereby rendered superfluous. Instead, an underworld containing all the infrastructure and parking space is created, together with a peaceful upper world for pedestrians. The technical world below is made possible the idyllic conditions above.
The principle of layering has been applied here to emblematic effect in four layers: underworld, deck, shops and dwellings. The deck is laid out as a continuation of the grid with an orthogonal pattern of streets that is nonetheless brusquely interrupted by a diagonal that connects two existing, dead-end shopping streets and transforms them into a shopping route. The retail concept is basic: there is place within the grid for big and small shops, according to demand, and the shopping route is simply the residual space between the blocks of shops. The housing programme is contained in a compact layer on the roof above the shops and comprises patio dwellings, and dwellings with roof garden and panorama room, all accessed by a network of streets on the roof.
Stacked one above the other like the layers of a cake, the different functions form a single megastructure in which all the uses are efficiently linked to one another by means of short, vertical connections while visual linkage is provided by openings and voids. In its emphasis on a congestive combination of all urban activities in one megastructure, the design is related to the metropolitan architecture of the 1960s rather than to the anti-urban tradition from which Almere is descended.

The designed form of OMA's vision for Almere's centre contained little that had been invented especially for this location. Strange as it seems, the ---> 56

47 The shopping streets in the competition plan are directly connected to the existing shopping streets and ensure that dead-ends become part of a continuous network of streets.

Pedestrian routes
The two main shopping streets in Almere-Stad are too far apart. Moreover, the older of the two streets is in a state of decline which threatens to affect the whole shopping centre with a sort of creeping gangrene. In our proposal therefore these two streets are incorporated into a strongly interwoven network of shopping routes and directly linked to one another by a diagonal connecting route running across the curved ground plane.

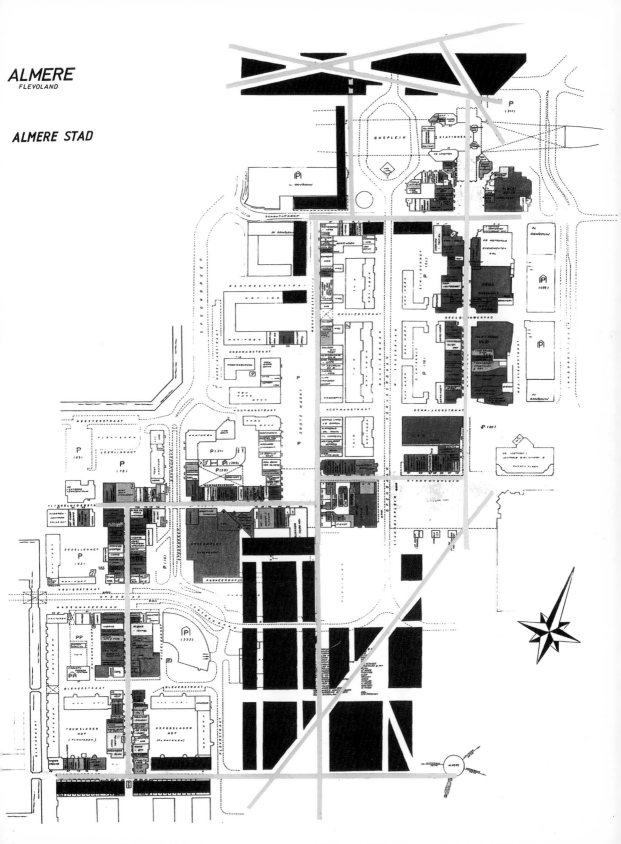

ALMERE
FLEVOLAND

ALMERE STAD

The office strip

We conducted a series of studies to see how a large number of office blocks could be brought together in the strip of land immediately behind the station. We tried using smaller offices as building blocks to create a larger mass and identity. What we were aiming for was a large concentration of volumes with a stratification of uses. Half sunken, obliquely situated car parks span the bus lane with their mass. On top of this is a public, slightly curved ground plane from which the lobbies of the various offices can be accessed. In a double layer above this are specialty shops, travel agencies, conference rooms, public and company restaurants, solicitor's offices and so on. Together these elements form a base for the various office towers.

The offices are organized in towers that are close enough to be linked to one another at various levels. This in turn gives rise to a greater variation in office depths and makes it possible to escape from the far-reaching standardization of Dutch office floor plans. The towers are tall enough to be visible from all over the city and as such they form a beacon marking the position of the city centre.

This clustering of offices makes it possible to achieve a strong common identity with the help of what are in themselves relatively modest volumes.

The existing station concourse will be enlarged and linked directly and on the same level with the circulation routes running over this office deck.

48 The site north of the station, dedicated area for the office strip.

49 First study of the office area near the station in the form of a continuous 'Manhattan grid'.

50 The principle of the curved ground plane at the office strip location, with below a two-level, obliquely sited car park.

51 Vertical view of the composition of the office strip.
1 Offices
2 Two floors of shared programmes for the offices (meeting and conference rooms, canteen, courier services, translation agency, copy shops, printer, bank and smaller rentable offices).
3 Retail deck with more or less office-related shops.
4 Raked car parks.
5 Bus lane.

52 The proposed composition of the office slabs.

53-54 Early studies for a further concentration of the required volume.

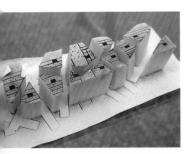

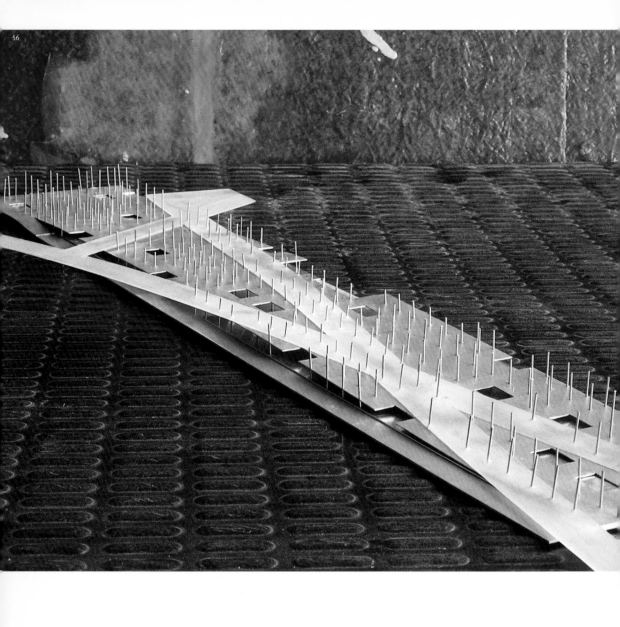

58

59

60

56 The public level on the ground plane is criss-crossed by a number of pedestrian routes.

57 The connective level, between the high-rise office towers, contains sufficient perforations to ensure an adequate supply of daylight to the levels below.

58/59 Studies for a further concentration of the required volume.

60 Final proposal for the organization of the volumes.

61 The office cores are so planned that they do not block the through routes.

62 A semi-public level containing various office-related functions develops above the public area.

63 Final composition of the office strip.

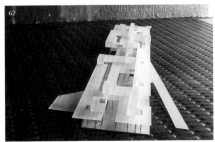

entire plan is a collage of features from the well-known OMA repertoire. The choice of congestion as the central design theme relies on the same hyperbole that had so impressed the mayor of Lille when Koolhaas presented that city with a similar plan. In Almere it was associated with the 'quantum leap' the city was currently engaged in and which would shortly make it truly 'great'. Seen from the perspective of OMA's oeuvre, it is not just the choice of congestion that is predictable but also the dialectical contrast in which that congestion is placed with 'emptiness'. Concentration of the programme so that elsewhere – in this case right beside the projected centre – a prior situation can be allowed to continue undisturbed for the time being, is unmistakably orthodox OMA.

OMA's city centre mixes infrastructure, public space, retail, leisure and residential uses in a compact, delicately contrived form. In the polder such a form has the shock of the new, but Koolhaas has been acquainted with this type of juxtaposition ever since his discovery of the Downtown Athletic Club in New York. Hybrid structures for shopping and amusement have been built in the American suburbs since the late 1960s and in Asia, too, the mixed-use building with vertical zoning is an everyday phenomenon.[16] Programmatically, therefore, the new Almere centre rests on a host of established types mediated by Koolhaas's own preoccupations. These preoccupations are accentuated in the stylistic articulation of the programme so that the 'personal' signature that characterizes many other OMA buildings (e.g. the conference centre in Agadir, the Urban Design Forum in Yokohama) is visible in Almere as well. Not for the first time, the real substance of the plan resides less in the elevations than in the sections. It is here that the mercurial mixture of now compatible, now antagonistic elements that has become OMA's hallmark, is brewed. The curved ground plan separates the 'upper world' from the 'underworld'. The sections, however, reveal more than a mere accumulation of discrete layers. Owing to the seemingly random subdivision pattern and the variation in gradients, incisions and spatial links, an exceptionally refined spectacle is achieved within the in itself well-organized shell of the triple-layered composition.

Allergy

In a departure from what we have come to expect from OMA, the practice's commentary on the Almere design contains no analytical studies, no density projections, no data compilations or cartoons, no infrastructural diagrams showing that Almere is actually at the centre of Europe. What is more, there is no narrative about Almere and no interpretation, no psychoanalysis of this eminently psycho-analysable city. What has become of the 'systematic idealization, the spontaneous exaggeration'[17] that characterizes so much of OMA's work? The inspiration for Almere-Centrum would appear to derive from a powerful allergy to Almere, to Dutchness in fact, rather than from any positive perception of the town. The plan is in a way an attack on everything that Almere is: Almere is low, the plan is high; Almere is a grid, the plan is full of diagonals; Almere is low density, the plan is high density. Above all it is determined to be different from Almere. Just as the police station ten years earlier was an allergic reaction to the architecture of Almere-Haven, so the centre plan was born out of an allergy to the provincial urbanity of Almere-Stad.

OMA explained its intentions as follows: 'Almere is a poly-nuclear agglomeration, traffic and zoning are hierarchic in a sixties fashion. The functional separation is maintained in the centre as well, which – in its form of a grid – fakes a 'traditional' city. Our proposal superposes pedestrians and buildings on top of all infrastructures, creating a density of public presence in the (new) centre that is contrasting the routine of suburbia. Researching possible urban block patterns, OMA defined the centre as a place "other" than the existing city in terms of density, spatial diversity and orientation to achieve a place of maximum public interaction.'[18] In the yet another paraphrase of Van Klingeren OMA proclaimed: 'Let Almere be a place of maximum public interaction!'.

Oddly enough it was the very otherness of OMA's plan that appealed to Almere's administrators. Even Almere, it seems, is allergic to Almere. The ambition of a young city, the sense of having to catch up, coupled with the aforementioned Dutch horror of being 'thought old-fashioned' exposed by ····⫸ 61

The rape seed strip

The competition brief drawn up by Almere city council was based on the assumption that all the remaining open areas in the centre would be fully used. One side-effect of our radical concentration of building volumes is that not all those areas need to be developed. This opens up the possibility of creating two parks, one beside the lake and the other to the north of the office strip.

In addition, the entire strip of land on the east side of the city centre can remain undeveloped and be set aside for the next generation. The act of leaving some areas in the centre undeveloped for the time being creates possibilities for the future. To symbolize the as yet untapped potential of this zone, we suggested that it should be sown with rape seed, the pioneer plant of the polder.

James Kennedy, together form an irresistible complex of arguments for supporting the plan.

For all that, it was largely due to the persuasive powers of Kor Buitendijk that OMA's plan, which had not started out as the jury's favourite, ended up being declared the winner. But not before it had undergone several modifications: the jury was worried about the slab of dwellings above the shops which evoked associations with the closed and covered shopping streets of Hoog Catharijne, the commercially successful but physically and psychologically intimidating 1960s shopping complex in Utrecht. With this spectre in mind, OMA was asked to alter the plan so as to dispel the risk of shadowy shopping arcades. The housing layer completing the megastructure would have to disappear for the plan to win.

OMA acquiesced, but since this altered the whole concept of the design, Floris Alkemade felt obliged to reexamine the principles of the curved ground plane. He considered many variations on the rigid pattern created by the diagonal transecting the blocks of shops on the deck. Together with Rob Hilz he drew a whole string of 'mock' morphologies in which the retail blocks were seemingly scattered at random across the deck in a parody of the grid. Only seemingly, because the diagonal pedestrian route across the deck had been retained, only in a less linear version, and several existing streets were carried through into the plan area. The dwellings were now placed above the individual blocks of shops.

 67

The presentation of the competition design

For the official presentation, our aluminium and coloured plastic models were mounted in an existing balsa-wood model of the city centre. The contrast in materials and the detailing on our models happened to emphasize mostly the large scale of our plan. The two areas of development were so totally different from the existing surroundings that it was as if two enormous space ships had landed in the city.

The jury was unable to reach a unanimous decision on the basis of the first round of design presentations. It accordingly decided to invite two of the four practices to respond to jury criticisms in a further development of their plans.

Criticism of our plan focused on the massiveness of the design and on the layer of dwellings above the shops.

The jury was afraid that the housing slab would turn the shopping level below into another 'Hoog Catharijne', a famous elevated and covered shopping centre in the heart of Utrecht which, though commercially successful, has never had a good popular image. The rest of the plan met with great enthusiasm.

66

67

66 Presentation model of office strip.

67 Presentation model of the carré.

68 First study aimed at making the residential level of the competition plan less massive.

69/70 The residential level is placed directly on top of the blocks of shops.

71/72 Modified competition plan in which the continuous residential level has disappeared.

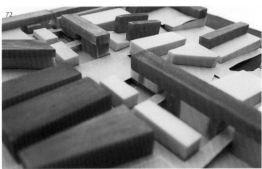

Since there was no convincing the jury that the comparison with Hoog Catharijne was totally unjustified, we looked for ways of making the housing layer less massive. We began by increasing the number of perforations and in a second version we placed the dwellings above the individual blocks of shops. Although this modification was enough to win us the competition, we were far from happy with it ourselves. A city centre with shopping blocks in grid formation at ground level topped by dwellings in the same configuration was too far removed from our original intentions. As such this was the first element to be altered when we came develop the plan further.

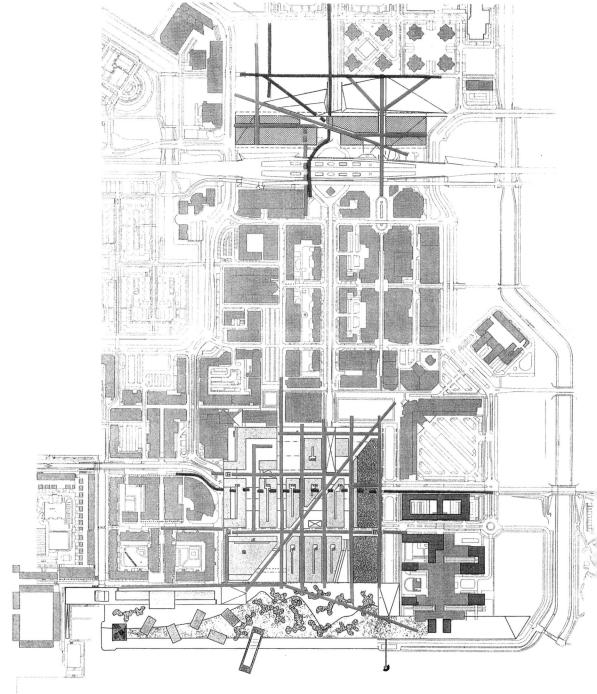

bicyclists

pedistrians

73 Orthogonally organized
pedestrian routes in the
competition plan.

74 Subdivision studies of the carré
with non-orthogonal arrangement of blocks.

Elaboration into masterplan

Because the dwellings now lay directly above the
blocks of shops, the block organization unintention-
ally set the tone for a major part of the plan.
For this reason the first thing we did in this elaboration
phase was to experiment further with the layout of the
shopping streets.
The fact that the roads and all car and goods traffic was
concentrated in the bottom layer meant that the
configuration of the upper layers did not have to take
account of the huge turning circles of manoeuvring
lorries. Since all the shops would be supplied from
below the deck, it became possible to make all-round
blocks without the usual rear entrances for goods
deliveries.

This made for considerable freedom in organizing the
curved ground plane. Studies were carried out into a
number of variants that exploited this freedom in
different ways.

At the express wish of the city council, the diagonal axis we had proposed was to form the basis of any new configuration.

A unique feature of this elaboration process were the fortnightly meetings with the city and the two developers involved (MAB and Blauwhoed Eurowoningen) at which we presented the fruits of our studies.

This enabled us to test the feasibility of our ideas immediately and allowed the city and the developers to help steer the design process. As a result, the elaboration of the design took on more and more the character of a joint venture.

That this set-up was no guarantee for a jointly supported plan became evident when MAB's growing doubts about the way the plan was developing blossomed into a full-blown crisis: after the summer break MAB presented the city with an alternative develop-ment plan produced in collaboration with another architectural office.

This interim phase eventually resulted in a ten point summary of MAB's objections to our plan. The critique focused on the status of the grid in the centre of Almere and on the various connections with the existing city centre and the lake.

In the ensuing discussions and a meticulous consideration of the ten points, the plan underwent yet another development from which it eventually emerged stronger than before.

The PPP game

Since the project was to be developed in a Public Private Partnership (PPP) the council now had the job of choosing a suitable property developer. They opted for the combination of Blauwhoed Eurowoningen, a developer specializing in housing, and MAB, which had built up quite a reputation for inner urban developments and for architecturally outstanding projects with a 'cultural' element, in particular with recent projects in The Hague (The Resident) and Eindhoven (De Heuvelrug). Blauwhoed would develop the dwellings, MAB the shops and cultural facilities and the council would take responsibility for public space and infrastructure. MAB, in the person of Mariet Schoenmakers, took an active part in the design process.

The choice of MAB amounted to an arranged marriage between the extraordinary (OMA) and the convivial (MAB), between the new and the familiar. It was an attempt to offset a perceived shortcoming of the idiosyncratic OMA, for as everyone knows 'OMA's plans are not convivial'.[19] The Almere council was represented in the PPP by the newly formed 'City Centre' department headed by the director of public works, Frits Helmig. The department was a veritable city within a city, with representatives from every municipal service from sewerage to land development, from lighting to public safety: all the expertise required to make a city united under one roof.

While a feasibility study was being conducted during 1995,[20] the two developers pondered their position vis à vis OMA's plan. MAB in particular harboured grave doubts about the collaboration with OMA and the quality of the plan. Some time in the summer of 1995 these doubts gave rise to what became popularly known as 'the MAB crisis': MAB made a countermove and decided to offer an alternative to OMA's megastructure.

They invited to Cesar Pelli, the American architect who had designed a tower block for MAB in The Resident, to show how it might be done differently. The Resident programme is not all that different from that of Almere-Centrum. It has an equally heavy office and housing component plus a tram line running right through the planning area. It has also had to deal with all

75 Study for an extra connection between the carré and the existing city.

76 Study for fine tuning the diagonal route, based on the street width requested by the developer.

77 Mariet Schoenmakers, urban designer with MAB.

77

the complications of building within an existing city. Yet in its resolution of these complications The Resident is in almost every respect the very antithesis of Almere-Centrum. The Resident, which is based on a masterplan by Rob Krier, employs tried and tested urban typologies: streets, squares and familiar architecture. Even an anonymous 1960s office tower already on site has been transformed by Michael Graves into something that looks like two classic Dutch houses. The Resident thus represents an enormous advance for postmodernism, which in its most sculptural, humorous and historicizing form had never managed to make much headway in the modernist stronghold of the Netherlands.

Pelli's alternative vision of Almere-Centrum pitted the familiar world of The Resident against the experimental curved ground plane of OMA. That summer, to defuse the crisis that had arisen, MAB, Blauwhoed, the project manager and the alderman responsible for the city centre, Cees van Bemmel, withdrew to the countryside for a weekend to consider the pros and cons of both plans. After much careful deliberation, OMA emerged as the winner. Notwithstanding the ideological and formal differences between MAB and OMA, there was general agreement about the program-

78 The players, l. to r.
M.T. Kooistra,
F.C.M. van Leeuwen,
J.B. Nieuwenhuizen,
C.W.J. van Bemmel,
W. van Zijl
and A.Th. Meijer.

79 The Resident, The Hague.

78

matic foundations of the plan which demonstrated the latter's superior experience in the wake of Euralille. From that moment onwards the developers were committed to the plan and constructive collaboration was the order of the day.

The first thing MAB did in September 1995 was to draw up a list of 10 points the masterplan should satisfy. Despite MAB's declared intention to collaborate constructively on the plan, these points still contained a good deal of fundamental criticism of OMA's plan and amounted to an implicit rejection of its most basic principles. The 10 points were as follows:

1 The grid/orthogonal structure

The starting point is the present grid structure in which the connection with the existing city finds expression. Deviations from the orthogonal structure are not excluded, provided they result in a clear increase in (spatial-functional) quality.

As far as shops are concerned, orientation, continuity and route formation are important factors in this context because they create different types of retail environment.

2 The curved ground plane (CGP)

The CGP must not be allowed to become a dogma. The idea as such is supported. Its size is the product of the urban design plan, not an overriding design principle to which everything else must yield. The form and edges/transitions must be designed in relation to new and existing development. In our view the CGP is simply a (smaller) part of the new centre, a 'raised plateau' that serves to distinguish the 'hot spot' Almere. P.S. Public safety!

3 The 'carré'

The new section should not be an autonomous 'fortress', unrelated to its surroundings. Old and new must be designed as a unity. On the other hand the new should contain a 'there' for Almere which may differ from the old.

4 The Waterfront

The city centre should derive its identity from its unique position beside the Weerwater. The city's waterside location is particularly important for the creation of an entertainment ambience, a more museum-related cultural environment and the residential environment.

5 A vista

The city centre enjoys a vista over the Waterfront and Weerwater: a balcony overlooking the water joined to a public space/park area that connects the heart of the city with the water.

6 Reserves and densification

There needs to be a vision/strategy for the future after 2005; an indication of which areas will change in line with an overall vision for the centre as a whole.

7 Parking

The car park must be a safe place; partitioning in accordance with upper-deck functions; orderly, no interminable expanse, etc. Vertical connections with upper-deck functions. Extra attention should be paid to artificial and natural lighting and the location of other functions besides parking, such as a supermarket and the like.

8 Shopping concepts

(See commercial strategy.) Thought should be given to new shopping (complex) concepts. Recent developments suggest there is good reason for doing so: the current mega-store/complex trend could be accommodated in

---

The Waterfront

The most important revisions made during this phase related to the connections with the existing city and a far more explicit involvement of the waterfront in the centre development. In the process, the waterfront area evolved into a mixed-use programme in which dwellings and shops were combined with a diverse entertainment programme. The original carré was extended westwards with a whole new entertainment area so that here too links with the existing city were much more direct.

To free this area for development the city decided to demolish two housing blocks of 133 dwellings so as to create space beside the lake for new public functions.

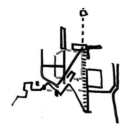
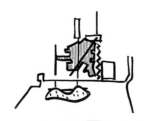

the centre of Almere rather than in some competing edge-of-town location. Provision should be made for poor weather conditions (wind, rain). A useful concept here is the comfortable, covered world of the 'shopping complex as a building within a building'.

In anticipation of the 'big city' it will be in 2005 Almere needs to create its own unique 'shopping experience' : a big shopping complex on the scale of the big city and an (architectural) 'grandeur' to match. As well as this there should of course be the 'ordinary good' shopping streets with dwellings above the shops.

9 Residential environment

A caring residential environment must be designed with a lot of attention to collective and semi-public areas. Another point to consider is the need to maintain a pleasant residential atmosphere at night in the midst of shut-up shops and closed/blank facades. The important thing is to create a variety of living environments which derive their strength from the different public spaces.

10 Changing colours

There must be an integrated design scenario for the development of the centre as a whole. On the basis of this plan the individual areas will then be labelled according to use, position in the street plan, atmosphere, spatial structure and type of public space.

In this integrated context old and new are seen as a single whole and a 'new reality' develops for both of them.[21]

OMA subsequently set about convincing MAB that their vision would satisfy all MAB's demands:

They showed how the grid continues across the curved ground plane.

They showed how a vista would be created from the curved ground plane to the water.

They showed how the programme above and below the curved ground plane could be connected by means of sunken and raised sections.

They showed how the curved ground plane was linked on all sides to the existing surroundings.

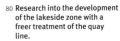

80 Research into the development of the lakeside zone with a freer treatment of the quay line.

They showed how a boardwalk along Weerwater connected the centre with the water.
They showed how indoor shopping conditions could be achieved by covering over residual spaces.

Masterplan

OMA reworked the plan into a masterplan that could be cast in a development plan. The masterplan took account of all the points discussed with all the parties concerned – council, traffic engineers, politicians, developers, shopkeepers, population.

Convivial: what MAB wanted above all else was a convivial centre, a centre capable of tempting people to 'go into town' without any particular purpose, such as happens in traditional cities. To illustrate what they meant they pointed to the development around the old harbour in Rotterdam where Piet Blom had conjured a 'historical' environment out of nothing (the area had been heavily bombed during the war). Not only was the area immediately adopted by Rotterdammers as a new entertainment district but it also became a tourist attraction owing to Blom's eye-catching 'cube dwellings'. This was the sort of environment required around Almere's Waterplein minus the small-scale architectural scene of the Rotterdam development: a twenty-first century type of conviviality.

Fabric: The second design Floris Alkemade made for the positioning of the shopping/housing blocks on the deck was welcomed by MAB who hailed this irregular and unpredictable pattern as a modern, scaled-up version of medieval urban fabric, with the same irregularity and unpredictability and the same degree of visual stimulus. The deck was beginning to look more and more like a traditional city.

Compact urbanity: OMA has opted here for a compact urban centre, in terms of both uses and form. The idea of centrality is translated here into high density, layering and mass. As Koolhaas puts it: 'All the models modernism has come up with for the notion of centrality have failed to deliver'.[22] Which

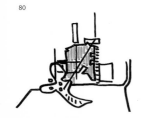

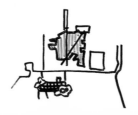

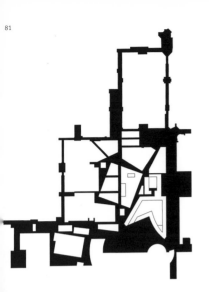

81 Pattern of public spaces dove-
    tails with the existing city.

82 Pattern of development relates
    to the existing urban fabric.

83 Zones where the ground plane
    is manipulated shown in white.

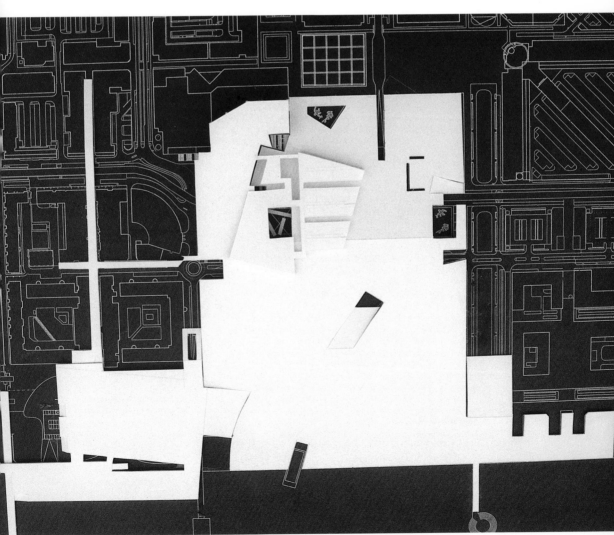

s why in Almere we find a city centre that is closer to the idea of the tradi-tional city than we would ever have expected from OMA. A greater contrast with the core-less, anonymous generic city, is difficult to imagine.

Underworld: The notion of 'conviviality' did not sit easily with the under-world of Almere-Centrum and MAB, fearful of a second Hoog-Catharijne, was seriously concerned about this part of the plan. Mariet Schoenmakers felt that OMA had adopted an unduly technocratic attitude, failing to realize that this concerned not just a technical system but the quality of the entire plan. She insisted that the number of openings in the deck be increased, thereby improving accessibility and averting the danger of a spooky underground cavern.

Shopping route: The discussions on the shopping route continued: according to the unwritten rules of retailing, a shopping route should be compact, with the store fronts a certain fixed distance from one another. MAB's strictures were based on its own developer's experience which had proved its worth in earlier projects.

Marketability: MAB, which has to be able to sell the shops to an investor, was concerned about stable value, durability and profitability. The new centre must not be a monument to the architect; it was there to be used. Disdain for shopkeepers, café owners and the general public was out of place. In the meantime, OMA continued to search for an alternative that would allow it to circumvent the iron laws of the developer.

Waterfront: OMA was required to bear in mind the appeal exerted by water even though it had never regarded the waterfront as the climax of the plan. Why should a view over water be more interesting than a view over the city? OMA reasoned. This of course went against the logic of the developers for whom the 'waterside location' is a useful selling point for their apartments. It also went against the logic of the city council who delight in advertising Almere as a waterside city.[23]

····> 82

84/85 Impressions of the new subdivision.

86 The Almere-Centrum Quality-team, l. to r. Maarten Schmitt, Rem Koolhaas, Tania Concko, Arnold Reijndorp.

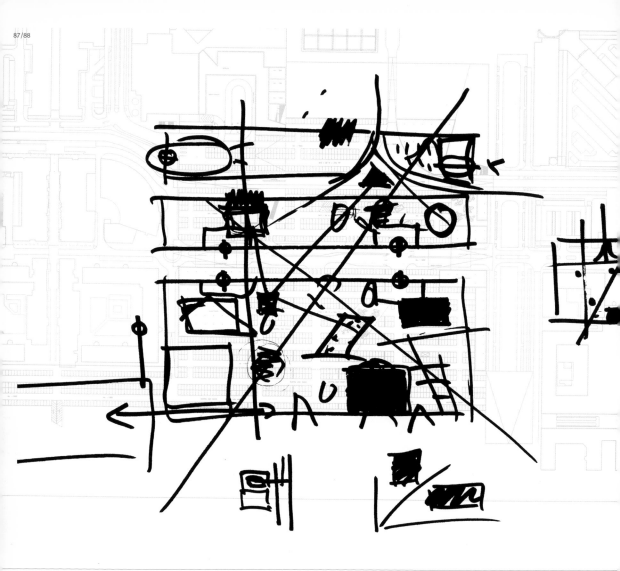

The 'underworld'

Most of the studies carried out during the process of
turning the competition design into a masterplan
related to the levels above the curved ground plane.
In the car-oriented level beneath the curved ground
plane the original ambitions remained virtually
unchanged.

In a number of modifications, this level, which was
perhaps the most interesting from our point of view,
acquired additional retail programme while the clarity
of its layout was augmented by linking all the vertical
access points to a single continuous pedestrian route.
Apart from keeping an eye on the elaboration and
quality of this layer, the council's chief concern was
our habit of referring to it as the 'underworld'.

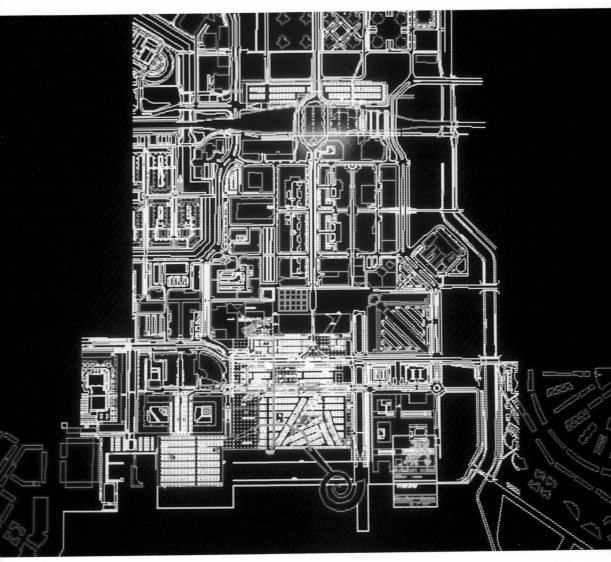

87 Car park level at the time of the competition.

88 Investigation into the possibility of adding new routes, shops and daylight openings to the car park level.

89 Car park slotted into existing surroundings.

90 Studies of horizontal and vertical entrance turns made by roads and bus lane.

91/92 Research model showing pattern of interventions in the car park.

90

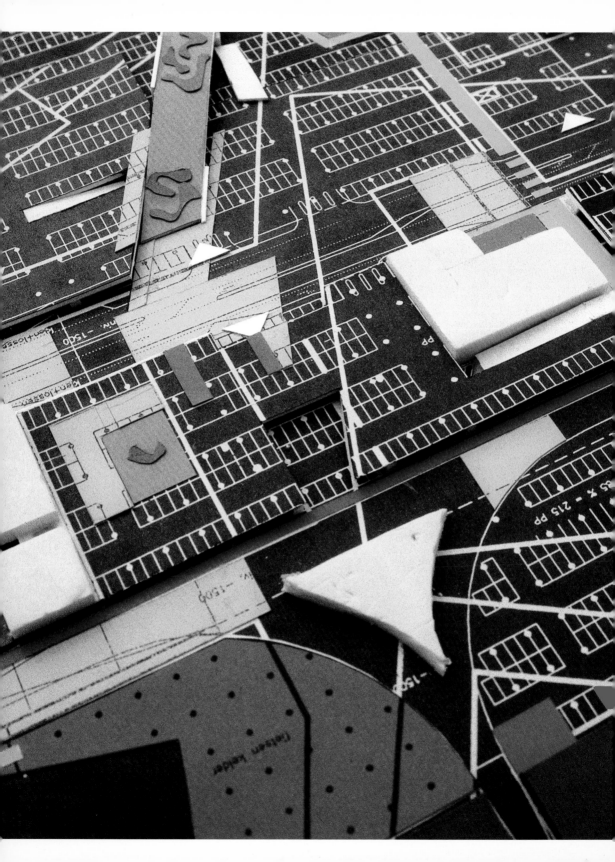

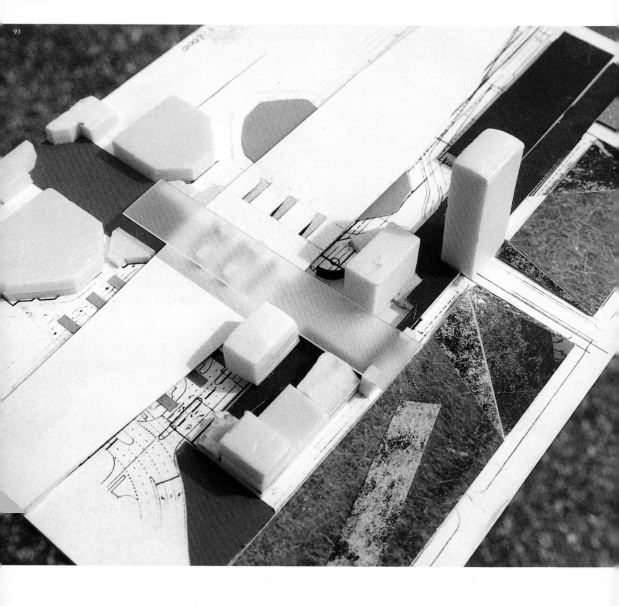

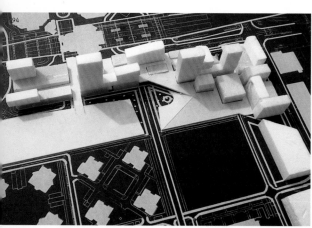

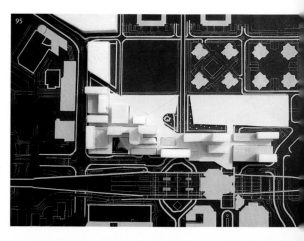

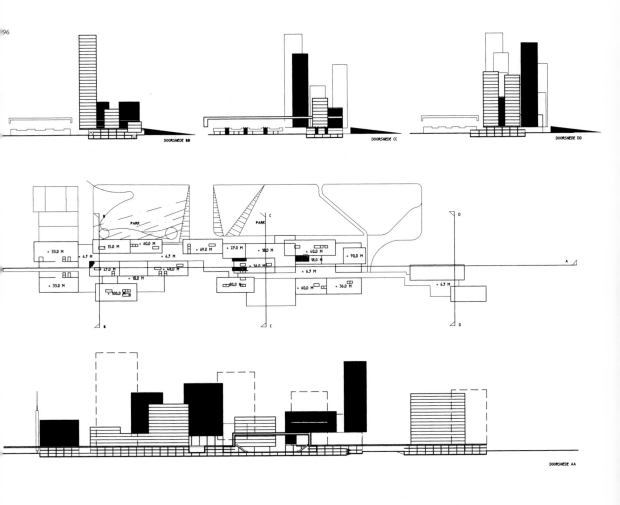

DOORSNEDE BB

DOORSNEDE CC

DOORSNEDE DD

DOORSNEDE AA

The office strip

The northern office strip also developed in relative
calm. Throughout this phase most of the attention was
focused on the southern section. The office strip was
developed without undue discussion, the most important change being the disappearance of the shared
level with a semi-public programme. This was at the
request of the council which did not want to burden
the developers of the various towers with all kinds of
requirements regarding connections they might not
even want. This level would also have seriously compli-
cated the phased development of the strip as a whole.

93 The existing tracks will be
augmented with an extra
platform. The existing station
concourse will be enlarged and
extended into the office strip.

94/95 Further elaboration of the
wings of the office strip and
connection with the park on top
of the raked ground plane.

96 Sections and elevations of the
offices.

First Pile

97/98 Integration of plan with the existing city.

99 Detail.

In May 1999 the first pile was driven for the Waterplein car park designed by OMA.[24]

1999

OMA rules

1999

Rem Koolhaas refers to the method OMA used to arrive at the masterplan as 'the Japanese model'[25]: in the course of endless, polite discussions and negotiations involving mutual give and take, the plan develops to everyone's satisfaction. In the Netherlands this 'Japanese' model is better known as the 'polder model', elsewhere as 'the Dutch way'. However allergic OMA may be to Dutchtown and Dutchness, there is no getting away from its roots. Though more practised in the conflict model, it appears that OMA is also perfectly at home with the polder model. Who would have thought it?

In December 1996 OMA was officially commissioned to turn its plan into a masterplan and in February 1997 a Quality Team was set up to oversee the development and advise the council as necessary. Led by The Hague city architect, Maarten Schmitt, the team consists of Rem Koolhaas, Spanish urban designer Manuel de Solà-Morales, Rotterdam urban sociologist Arnold Reijndorp, and the young French architect Tania Concko.
OMA's solution for the centre of Almere was in fact more in the nature of a building than a spatial framework. As such it did not provide a flexible framework for scattered and somewhat discrete initiatives around a neutral collective zone. The building that was to become Almere's city centre needed to be very finely orchestrated indeed if it was to fulfil the intentions of the ground plan and the section. This explains Koolhaas's keen interest in the choice of architects, for the plan stands or falls with the architectural interpretation. With his appointment to the Q-team Koolhaas hoped to safeguard the interpretation of the plan and the choice of architects. It was at his instigation, for example, that the Japanese architect Kazuyo Sejima was among the archi- ····} 86

Oddly enough the biggest problem after this phase was the fact that enthusiasm for the plan among all the parties was now so great that it threatened to become an obstacle to further modification.
Now that a general consensus had been reached the city council in particular was keen to freeze the plan in this form. For our part, we considered it essential that it should remain possible to alter the plan in response to all kinds of as yet unforeseeable developments. We regarded the contribution of the various architects who would be designing the different blocks as particularly important for ensuring that the plan had sufficient consequence.

tects invited to produce a design for one of the most crucial buildings in the plan, the theatre in the lake.

OMA has a lot more power and say in the implementation of Almere centre plan than urban designers in the Netherlands usually enjoy on such mega-projects. This is probably a reflection of their experience of complex urban design situations, such as Euralille: OMA knows the ropes.
OMA's strong position is all the more remarkable given that after its initial design had been accepted as the basis for further development, it was not at all certain that OMA would be involved in the making of a masterplan. Yet the office managed to maintain its position, sometimes through endless meetings, sometimes by giving way, sometimes by putting its foot down, and sometimes by virtue of the threatening letters fired off by Rem Koolhaas from one or another of his temporary Asian residences.

The elaboration of the first phase area

When it came to implementation of the plan, the politicians were keen to see work start not on the town hall side of the site, but in the opposite corner beside the lake. They intended in this way to give fresh impetus to the area in most urgent need of change.
The programme for this first phase area consists of a mix of housing, shops, a hotel and a varied entertainment programme with restaurants, bars, a discotheque, theatre, multiplex cinema, bowling alley, fitness centre and pop concert hall.
This first phase area is part of the continuous waterfront development and can at the same time be read as an extension of the original 275 m by 275 m carré. Whereas the carré has a curved ground plane, this first phase area has a car park under a raised but flat

ground plane. The floor of this car park is level with the water level in the lake. One whole side of the car park looks out over the lake.
In this phase we added a sunken events plaza to the design. The plaza is on the same level as the car park and opens into a similarly sunken garden that accompanies a public route through the car park. In this area, too, the doubling of the ground plane makes it possible to access the various programmes on two levels.
In the car park, a higher ceiling and a different soffit treatment below the buildings reveals the contours of the superstructure above. In effect, the layout of the upper world is made legible in the car park below, thereby simplifying orientation still further.

The Underworld

The evocative term *dynamique d'enfer* (a dynamic from hell), coined during the work on OMA's first big urban scheme, Euralille, suggested intense, 'infernal' complexity. That complexity applied to the object of contemporary urban development, that is to say to the programme and the design, but to a much lesser degree to the process. In Lille the key players — mayor, businessmen and designers — were behind the plan *en bloc*, at least if we are to believe Rem Koolhaas's account. Indeed, it was one of the officials involved in this project who described why the plan had to be so infernal. It was because the city at the end of the twentieth century, unlike at the beginning, could no longer make do with 'generalizations'. Instead it demanded 'hyper-specific' solutions in an extremely dynamic pattern: 'So complex become all the interconnections, the mutual dependencies, the proliferation of interfaces, the superimposition of users and owners that together they form a group of prisoners, shackled by mutual obligation, exacerbated by the very complexity that you offered unwittingly.'[26] Just as Koolhaas had understood the geopolitical impulses behind the mayor of Lille's attempt to present this provincial town as the centre of Europe, so he could empathize with the partners who detected in complexity the most important cultural task of the moment. The opportunistic position of the surfer on top of the waves, which Koolhaas sought since the beginning of his career, proved profitable in Lille. Evidently there was complete agreement regarding the aims and content of the urban programme, irrespective of whether the agenda served politics, the design or big money.

In Almere, too, the thrust of the project was determined in the same unanimous manner — at least, once the various parties had accepted the fact that they were all in it together and there was no turning back. The Almere planning process is a classic example of the polder model in which all the parties attempt to serve their own interests through negotiation and discussion. Yet OMA's masterplan for Almere's new centre was far from being a typical product of consensus urban planning.

100 The Piranesian space in OMA's design for Euralille.

101 Study of entertainment area with development of a sunken aquatic square.

102 Study of the two levels of the entertainment area with car park and aquatic square on the lower level and above them the deck with indentations indicating location of buildings.

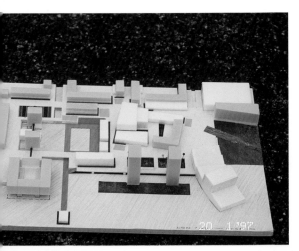

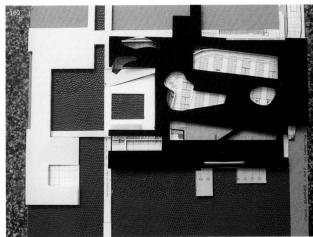

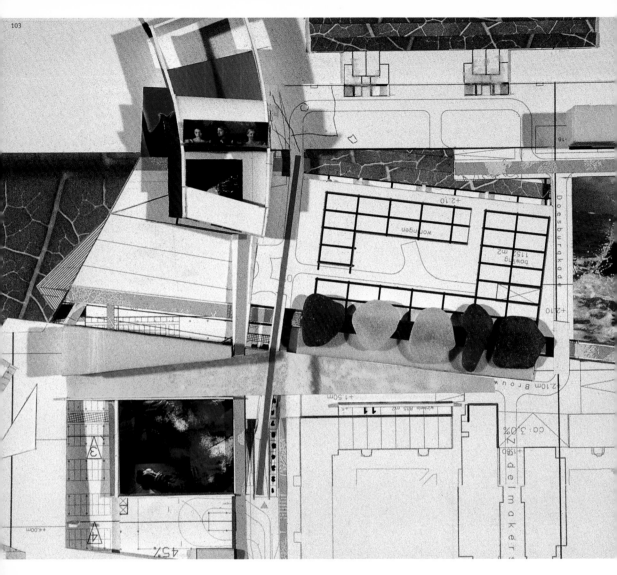

The development of the plan on the ground plane was a good test case for demonstrating the advantages of an open planning process. It had always been our intention that individual architects should, if they so wished, be allowed to develop their building in a way that might also impact on the elaboration and interpretation of the plan as a whole.

In selecting the various architects, therefore, an attempt was made to achieve a certain coherence that would work to the benefit of the plan.

In the first phase area William Alsop in particular asked for and was given considerable leeway for a completely different interpretation to the block assigned to him. The competition held for the theatre/cultural centre was ultimately won by Kazuyo Sejima (Saana) in collaboration with Greiner & Van Goor Architecten. Their mysterious transparent orthogonal design repre-

sents a further enrichment of the plan.

Various parts of the plan are now under construction. In the office strip the outer edges are being tackled first. Almere has succeeded in winning a WTC licence and bureau Urhahn is currently developing the middle section of the office strip for this purpose, largely in line with the original intentions of our plan. The biggest challenge at the moment is the final elaboration of the proposals for the totally refurbished station concourse to be realized in collaboration with Dutch Rail.

Construction has also begun in the southern section of the new city centre. All the buildings in the first phase area have been assigned to an architect, thus adding a steady stream of building designs to the masterplan. A firm of landscape architects (DS) has been engaged for the elaboration of the public realm. Working in close

Unlike the recent plans for the ritzy South Axis location in Amsterdam, for example, Almere is not a shapeless design that can be stretched every which way during the planning process. OMA's centre plan does not rest on a single civil engineering idea filled out with the precise (but architecturally fortuitous) outcome of the poker game between the various partners concerning the numbers and combinations of the programme. The fact of the matter is that OMA's plan had a definite form from the word go, a form that was sufficiently tough to resist the impact of all the tactical questions, market analyses, questions of political feasibility and vetos thrown at it during the design process.

Did the fact that OMA had designed an urban quarter as one enormous, faceted building perhaps mean that it was responding to Leon Battista Alberti's ancient exhortation to view the 'state' and the 'house' as interchangeable, interconnected quantities, a notion somewhat more recently defined by Aldo van Eyck as an interchangeability of 'city' and 'house'? In Van Eyck's teaching it was: 'make of every house a small city and of every city a large house'. OMA does indeed conceive Almere's city centre as 'a big house', but it is highly doubtful whether that choice was inspired by the same kind of assumptions about idealistic wholeness and universal reciprocity in which the humanist Van Eyck put his faith. OMA's urban house serves not so much to illustrate a similarity with the surrounding streets, squares and buildings, as to define an autonomous zone which, though accessible to the outside world, is nonetheless demarcated with facades, house styles and a whole range of other architectural details and which in no time at all, simply by closing a few doors, could even become completely self-supporting.

Almere's city centre offers no public space in the traditional sense. What it offers are the kind of particularized spaces we have come to know so well from North America where the public realm is almost synonymous with fear and insecurity. Just as in the shopping malls in the American suburbs, every square metre in Almere's centre has been functionally,

103 Study of feasibility of an open connection between the sunken levels of the aquatic square, the car park and the waterfront.

104-106 General models showing current development of the entertainment area.

legally and architecturally assigned so that no one need feel displaced — indeed, this aspect might well explain the success of OMA's plan in political and commercial circles. The autonomous nature of the centre has been further emphasized by the setting up of a special department to look after the management, security and cleaning. Rather than a subversive action on the part of a practice with a critical social agenda, the centre plan is, thanks to a reassuring set of qualities, wholly in line with current political and commercial practice. It seems that the surfer has once again chosen the most opportune sequence of waves.

It is interesting that it should be Koolhaas of all people, who used to complain that his Dutch colleagues were incapable of leaving parts of the spatial order empty and were naturally disposed to fill everything with form and colour, who has now abandoned the only neutral zone still to be found here and there in the Dutch city: the public realm.[27] Almere appears to have provided the ideal context for a fundamental readjustment of the notion of public space in today's cities, without automatically reiterating the paranoid urban models from North America or Asia. OMA's plan, which at the time of the competition in 1994 had the fairly autonomous and pure concept of a three-level megastructure, assimilated during the discussions with the market operators and the council. The design's form was not hard but elastic. The plan abandoned its autistic quality and now merges smoothly with its context; it contains an efficient shopping route in accordance with developers' norms; it creates an attractive waterfront according to the rules of urban design; it forms a striking skyline in keeping with the rules of city marketing and provides an attractive business centre consistent with commercial standards. One part of the plan has continued in various ways to evade the innocuous urbanity of the shopping centre, and that is the underworld. The name alone suggests a different atmosphere, which is why all the parties, with the exception of OMA, stubbornly persist in referring to it as the 'lower world'. Whereas the buildings on the deck and around the curved ground plane will be contracted out to other architects, the

collaboration with the city council and OMA they will address themselves to the design and layout of the ground plane.
Now at last it is the turn of the original core of the competition design, the grand carré. The last building of the first phase makes up one corner of the carré and the intention is that design work on the remaining blocks should begin in 1999. In a continuing process between now and 2005, the entire plan will eventually take shape.

underworld is OMA's domain. It is here that OMA's hidden agenda manifests itself.

107-110 Early studies for the level below

This is the place where OMA's affinity with the freedom and indeterminacy of the 1960s is most visible and where Van Klingeren, albeit in an infernal version, puts in an appearance. Enable more by doing less, inspiration based on imperfection – this is the kind of association the design of the underworld evokes. The designers clearly opted here for emptiness instead of fullness, for the freedom of the blank space rather than the cosiness of horror vacui. The 1960s are present in the person of Van Klingeren rather than Van Eyck. The main absentee of course is the cheerfully playing homo ludens who would have populated an Almere designed by Van Klingeren. In OMA's underworld we sense the can't-touch-me aloofness of Espace Piranesien, a space made not for pedestrians but for cars, lorries and buses and whose layout reflects the technocracy of traffic and transport. The design is indicated by lines on the road, signs and pavements, symbols from a completely different universe than the urban design-regulated upper world.

For the keen-eyed sleuth there is yet another rudiment of the 1960s to be found in the underworld, one that can be traced back to architects usually characterized as technocratic, modernist formalists, such as Lucas and Niemeijer, Holt and Bijvoet, Van den Broek & Bakema and of course Maaskant; architects who even in their most formal commissions did not hesitate to incorporate utilitarian design methods and elements. They made spaces that seemed to have been designed not by architects but by engineers and which, far from wanting to elude a certain lugubriousness or eeriness even derived their sensation from it. How this is to be reconciled with the current emphasis on social safety is a moot point, but the fact remains that these sensations widen the range of the architectonic experience enormously and do in fact contribute to 'the complete city' which inevitably includes fear, negativity and forbidden and dark sides. Such spaces have a certain nonchalance and a freedom that fascinates because it invites a different experience and a different – conditioned – behaviour.

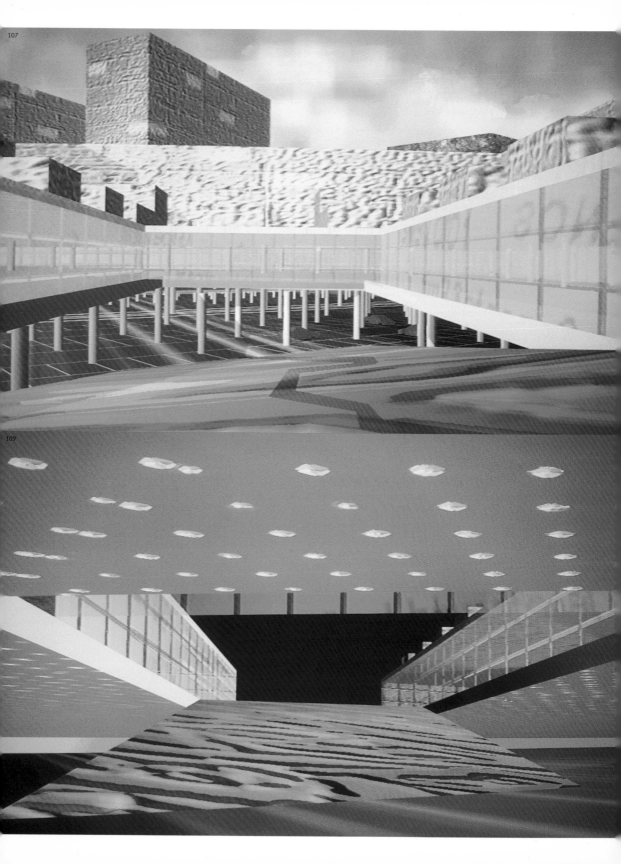

The underworld is OMA's attempt to design something that cannot be designed, to keep something exciting and blank and unpredictable, to make a 'playing field' for the contemporary urbanite.

In this context one is reminded of the 'urban planning design' Joep van Lieshout made for Almere in 1998 in the form of an autarkic farm, self-sufficient to the point of having its own artillery workshop and abattoir. Like OMA's plan it was of course a disgusted reaction to the petty bourgeois values and conformity of the middle-class paradise of Almere. Into a city where everything is regulated, where only happy families live and where the semblance of suburban bliss prevails, Joep van Lieshout introduced the counterforces of aggression, sex, alcohol and violence. The dullness of the suburb was challenged by introducing negative forces. In real-life Almere they do not need to be introduced for they are already present, they are just not visible. They need to be organized, as Kor Buitendijk intended. That, too, is part of 'the complete city'.

OMA parried the concern of the other parties regarding the character of the underworld with understatements and judicious rhetoric (actually, the underworld was 'more of a showroom than a car park') and with layered drawings full of light and air even in the lowest regions. It might perhaps have bolstered its argument by invoking eighteenth-century architectural theory since this was a period when the variety of architectonic sensation that seems to fascinate Koolhaas so much received a lot of attention. He might, for instance, have invoked his predecessor of two centuries ago, Nicolas Le Camus de Mézières, and his studied reflections on light and shadow: 'Light and shade artfully disposed in an architectural composition reinforce the desired impression and determine the effect. A building that is well lit and well aired, when all the rest is perfectly treated, becomes agreeable and cheerful. Less open, more sheltered, it offers a serious character; with the light still more intercepted, it becomes mysterious or gloomy.'[28] OMA drew and moulded this whole programme of sensations into a single building.

ses and cars will drive via openings beneath the curved ground plane to a 'parking cathedral' that will indeed be 'mysterious and gloomy' wing to lofty storey heights rising to as much as five metres and intermittent shafts of light admitted by the various voids. The buildings that scend through the ground plane are accessed via lighted doorways that ckon as invitingly as safety islands between the endless parking bays. om the motorway you will drive straight into the underworld, park your hicle and ascend to the upper world via the lower entrance of an apartment building, shop or cinema. Colour, light, designed columns and green rdens on the bottom of the underworld all go to make up a magical orld that might one day prove to be the real attraction of Almere-ntrum.

Notes

1 The following passage about urban renewal is based on: Crimson, Re-Urb. Nieuwe plannen voor oude steden, Rotterdam 1997.
2 James C. Kennedy, Nieuw Babylon in aanbouw. Nederland in de jaren zestig, Amsterdam 1995.
3 Petra Brouwer, Van stad naar stedelijkheid. Planning en planconceptie van Lelystad en Almere 1959-1974, Rotterdam 1997.
4 Quoted in: Bernard Hulsman, 'Protesten tegen de sloop De Meerpaal', NRC Handelsblad, 20 July 1999.
5 In 1999 Dronten town council voted to demolish the Meerpaal and build a multi-cultural centre on the site. In fact the building's concept had been wrecked back in the 1980s with the partitioning and renovation of the interior.
6 Martijn de Rijk, 'Almere. Een nieuw stad, is dat haalbaar?', Haagse Post 20, 18 May 1974.
7 Two newspapers in particular, Haagse Post and Nieuwe Linie, criticized everything to do with Almere.
8 Maarten Kloos, in Het Parool, 9 April 1992, p. N5.
9 Coen van der Wal, In Praise of Common Sense. Planning the Ordinary. A Physical Planning History of the New Towns in the IJsselmeerpolders, Rotterdam 1997, p. 229.
10 Idem, pp. 219-221.
11 'World Trade Center in Almere', Nieuwsbrief Dienst Stadscentrum 1998 no. 10. In OMA's plan the WTC will be in the business centre behind the station.
12 Richard Ingersoll, 'The lost horizon of new towns: The Woodlands and Almere in the metropolitan sprawl', Casabella, no. 614, 1994, p. 22.
13 Centrum Almere 2005. Nota van uitgangspunten, Almere 1994, p. 29.
14 Ibid., p. 13.
15 This team consisted of: Kor Buitendijk, external project manager for Stadscentrum, Brans Stassen, urban designer with the local authority, A.W.J.M. Cremer, external marketing consultant and E.P.J. Lemkes-Straver from the city development department.
16 For American prototypes of OMA's hybrid typology see: Peter G. Rowe, Making a Middle Landscape, Cambridge/London 1991, pp. 130-133.
17 Wouter Deen, Udo Garritzman, 'OMA's little helper', Arch+, no. 143, 1998, p. 72.
18 'Almere Urban Development', El Croquis, no. 79, 1996, p. 241.
19 Interview with Floris Alkemade, May 1999.
20 The feasibilitystudy was carried out from February 1995 to January 1996, by Pieters projects bureau.
21 'De tien punten van MAB', MAB archives.

The design team

Rem Koolhaas, Floris Alkemade

Olga Aleksakova
Juliette Bekkering
Frans Blok
Gro Bonesmo
Hans Cool
Donald van Dansik
Richard Eelman
Angelique Haver
Rob Hilz
Philip Koenen
Paul Kroesse
Rob de Maat
Margret Muller

Oresti Sarafo Poulos
Stijn Rademakers
Marcus Schaeffer
Karen Shanski
Jaakko van het Spijker
Enno Stemerding
Bas Suykerbuik
Luc Veeger
Heidi van der Wart

22 Interview with Rem Koolhaas and Floris Alkemade, July 1999.

23 'Het plan. Almere, stad aan het water', Almere 1997.

24 On the basis of the masterplan, the city council, MAB and Blauwhoed have entered into a joint venture - the 'Ontwikkelingscombinatie Almere Hart CV' - for a period of ten years. The developers bear the commercial risks; the council is responsible site preparation, infrastructure and public space but not the public buildings which will as far as possible be realized by the developers.

25 Interview with Rem Koolhaas and Floris Alkemade, July 1999.

26 Rem Koolhaas, S, M, L, XL, Rotterdam/New York 1995, p. 1208.

27 Rem Koolhaas, introduction in: Bernard Leupen, Wouter Deen, Christoph Grafe (eds.), Hoe Modern is de Nederlandse Architectuur?, Rotterdam 1990, p. 15.

28 Nicolas Le Camus de Mézières, The Genius of Architecture; or: The Analogy of that Art With Our Sensations, Santa Monica 1992 (1780), p. 88.

Architecture

In May 1999 work began on the construction of the OMA-designed car park beside Waterplein (aquatic square). It marked the start of the realization of the first phase of Almere-Centrum and of a construction process that will continue for many years to come. A number of the buildings planned for the new city centre are documented here. Many plans are still at the 'working design' stage and even the more advanced plans are likely to undergo some degree of modification. As such, this presentation is a snapshot of one moment in the dynamic process of building the city centre.

1   Theatre with Centre for Cultural Education
2   Urban Entertainment Centre (pop centre, shops and hotel)
3   Apartment buildings
4   Apartment building 'Silverline'
5   Student flats
6   Housing block
7   Multiplex cinema supermarket, shops, megastores, restaurants and parking
8   Car park entertainment area
9   Public realm
10 ICT businesses and 'Alnovum' Institute
11 'De Vlinder' Office building
12 'Le nouveau jour' Office building
13 Study for WTC

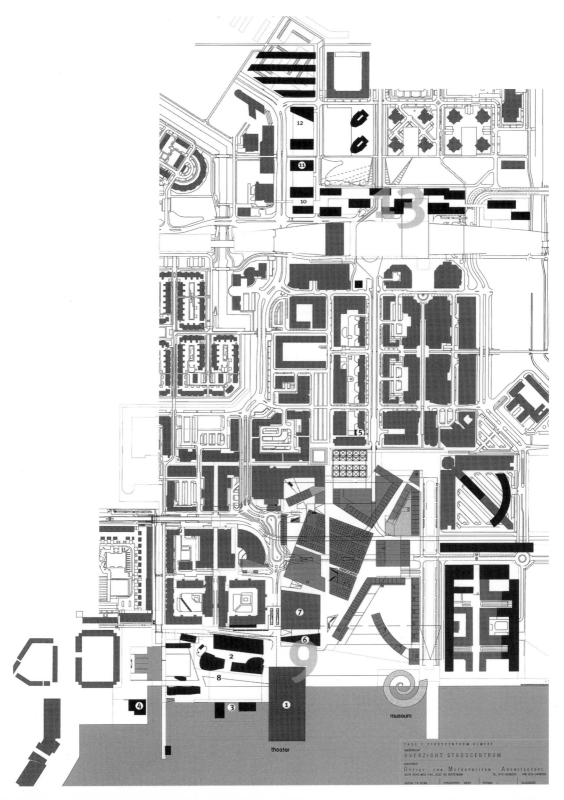

theater

museum

FASE 1 STADSCENTRUM ALMERE
ONDERWERP
OVERZICHT STADSCENTRUM
ARCHITECT
OFFICE FOR METROPOLITAN ARCHITECTURE
HEER BOKELWEG 149, 3032 AD ROTTERDAM   TEL 010-2438200   FAX 010-2438207
DATUM 14.10.99   PROJEKTNR 9333   SCHAAL —   BLADZIJDE

Theatre with Centre for Cultural Education

architect: Wiel Arets Architect & associates
client: Almere City/ MAB

Wiel Arets Architect & associates places the hybrid programme of theatre/Centre for Cultural Education in a stacked volume (vertical) along the water line (horizontal). The centrally located entrance (good connection with the city centre) allows for interchange between the particular conditions of an arts centre and the universal model of an opera/concert hall.

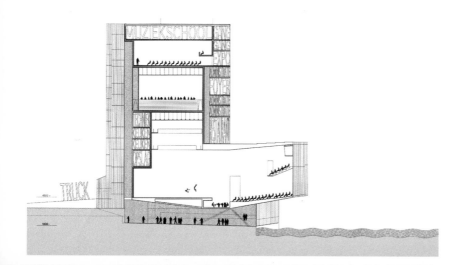

Theatre with Centre for Cultural Education

architect: MVRDV
client: Almere City/ MAB

MVRDV sees the combination of theatre/Centre for Cultural Education stipulated in the brief as an opportunity to furnish Almere-Stad Centre – a theme park of urban prototypes – with a production hall or 'artistic production plinth'. Three auditoria make up the structural support for the plinth in which and on which the cultural programme is located.

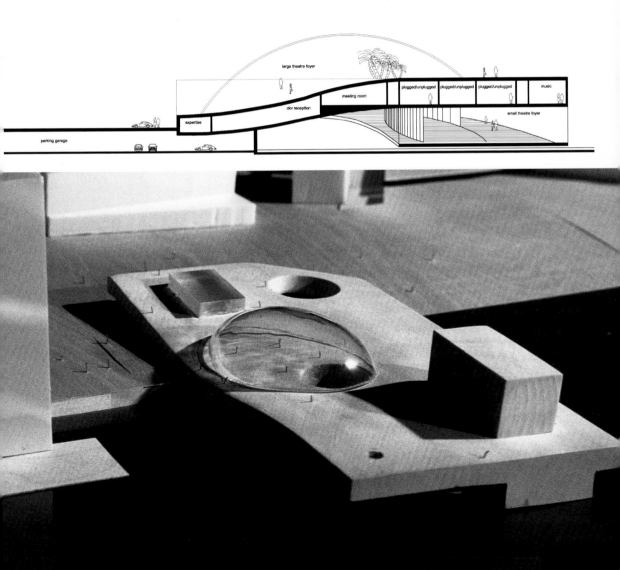

Theatre with Centre for Cultural Education

architect: Neutelings Riedijk Architecten
client: Almere City/ MAB

Neutelings Riedijk Architecten combines the two programmes (theatre and Centre for Cultural Education) into a single 'House of the Arts'. The public zone of the new city centre culminates in a set of characteristic 'Spanish steps' that are repeated inside the building. The gradually ascending 'hill town' is organized into three zones: auditoria, foyers and terrace.

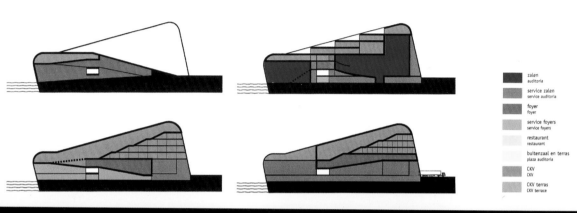

zalen
auditoria

service zalen
service auditoria

foyer
foyer

service foyers
service foyers

restaurant
restaurant

buitenzaal en terras
plaza auditoria

CKV
CKV

CKV terras
CKV terrace

Theatre with Centre for Cultural Education

Architect: Studio Libeskind
Client: Almere City/ MAB

Studio Libeskind seizes on Almere-Stad's redefinition of its centre as an opportunity to rethink the typology of the theatre. The ensuing deconstruction of the conventional concentric and introvert model, the Globe, results in a dynamic urban podium, Wave Orpheus, that involves the audience in the spectacle rather than leaving them sitting in the dark.

Theatre with Centre for Cultural Education (Chosen design)

architect: Greiner & Van Goor Architekten with SANAA Ltd/ Kazuyo Sejima, Ryue Nishizawa & Ass.
client: Almere City/ MAB
construction: 2001-2003

The winning design for the theatre and Centre for Cultural Education by Greiner & Van Goor Architekten with SANAA Ltd/ Kazuyo Sejima, Ryue Nishizawa & Ass. organizes the combination of uses in a single layer level with Weerwater lake. Rather than being linked by conventional corridors, the various spaces flow into one another without any sense of hierarchy, separated by transparent walls or intervening lobbies. The theatre itself is based on the principle: 'To bring as many people as possible as close as possible to the action on the stage and, consequently, to the actors.'

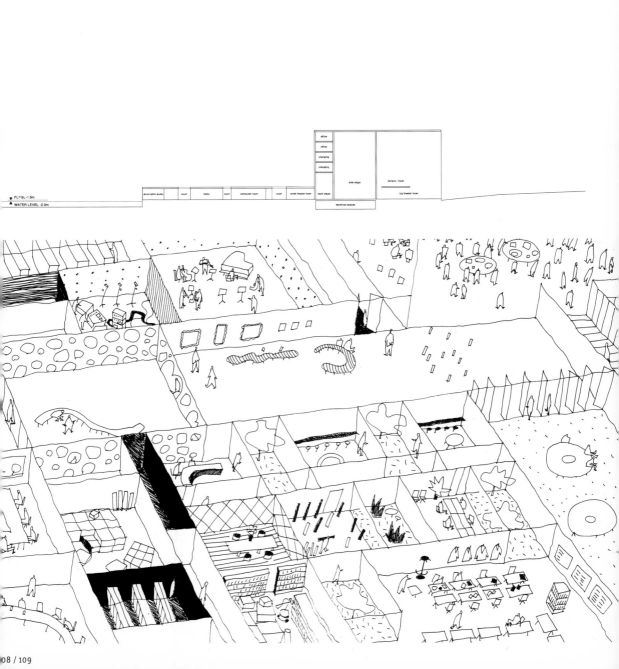

office
office
changing
changing

side stage

terrace / foyer

FL=GL-1.5m

WATER LEVEL -2.0m

drum/rythim studio   court   lobby   court   computer room   court   small theater foyer   back stage

big theater foyer

technical spaces

Urban Entertainment Centre (pop centre, shops and hotel)

architect: Alsop & Störmer Architects
client: MAB
construction: from 1999

shopping block

café on aquatic square

pop centre   disco   hotel

shopping block pop centre urban wall

hotel

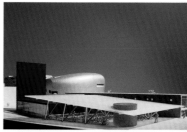

urban wall   bicycle garden

Student flats

architect: KoersZeinstraVanGelderen Architecten
client: Woningbouwvereniging Groene Stad Almere
construction: starts in 2000

An unexpected gap near Stadhuisplein (the result of faulty measurement) will be filled with the first eight student flats in Almere-Stad. KoersZeinstraVanGelderen Architecten drew inspiration for their design from the variety of 1980s bay windows, balconies, windows, entrances, baffles, lower fronts, loggias and porches to be seen in the city centre. The result is a building that subtly acknowledges and comments on the existing townscape.

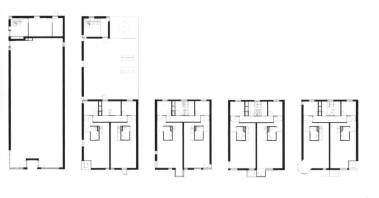

Apartment buildings

architect: de Architekten Cie.
client: Blauwhoed Eurowoningen
construction: from 1999

Two high-rise apartment buildings designed by Architekten Cie. are to be built beside Weerwater lake, in the middle of the new cultural centre. The residents will have the best of all worlds: a modern urban environment on their doorstep plus views over the polder landscape and a marina.

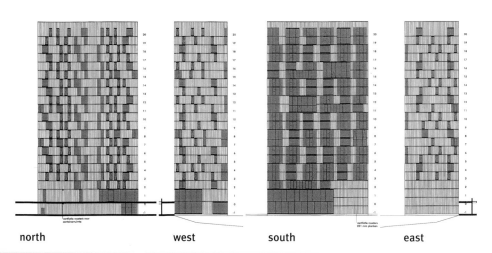

north   west   south   east

Apartment building 'Silverline'

architect: Claus & Kaan Architecten
client: Blauwhoed Eurowoningen
construction: from 1999

Apartment building 'Silverline', design by Claus en Kaan Architecten, is part of OMA's centre plan but is situated just across the canal in the existing urban structure. This ambivalence is one of the themes of the building which is right on the edge of the Stedenwijk quarter. The building's silhouette reflects the square-metre market value: the (expensive) top and bottom levels are massive while the (cheaper) intermediate volume is slender.

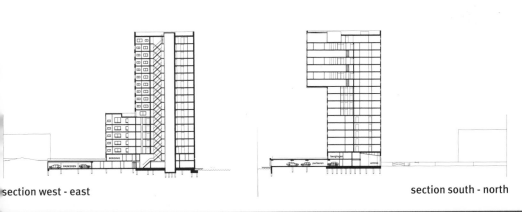

section west - east
section south - north

Housing block

architect: Van Sambeek & Van Veen Architecten
client: Eurowoning/MAB
construction: from 2002

Situated at the head of the cinema/retail block and separated from it by a narrow street, is a housing block, designed by Van Sambeek & Van Veen Architecten. The building is a three-dimensional puzzle of circulation and different dwelling types. On the side facing the water and the park a facade of movable glass panels encloses winter gardens.

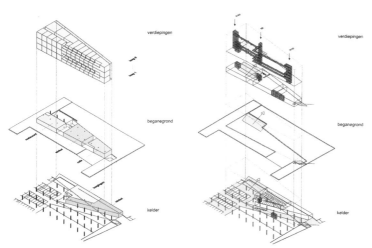

Multiplex cinema, supermarket, shops, megastores, restaurants and parking

architect: Office for Metropolitan Architecture
client: MAB
construction: 2001-2002

This building - the first block to be built on the carré - occupies a special position. It fulfils a pioneering role in that it demonstrates the possibilities offered by the carré for accessing buildings both via the car park and via the deck. The varied programme ensures that the block will be used in different ways throughout the day.

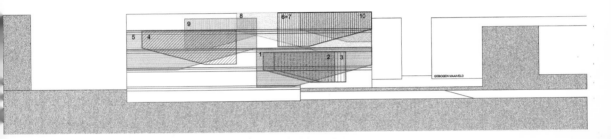

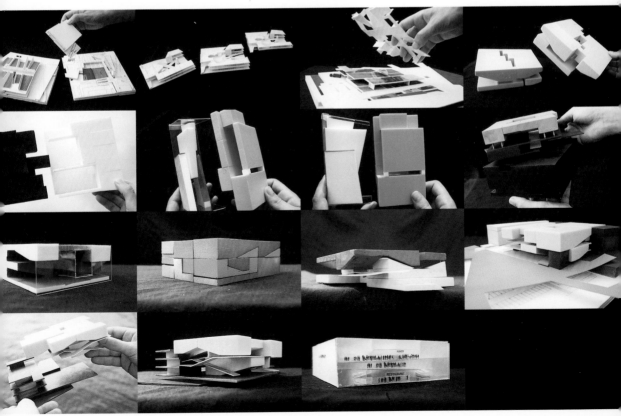

Car Park entertainment area

architect: Office for Metropolitan Architecture
client: Almere Hart CV
construction: begun in May 1999

The single-storey car park is on the same level as Weerwater and one long side looks out over the lake. On top of the car park are various buildings (whose footprints can be read in the car park ceiling) and the entertainment zone. The sunken car park provides same-level access to the theatre forecourt and the aquatic square. The car park is divided into a residents' and a public section that are separated by a garden.

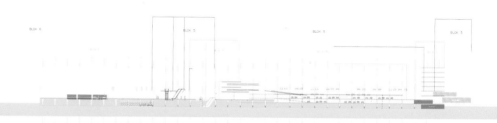

Public realm

architect: DS landschapsarchitekten
client: Almere City
construction: from 1999

On the basis of OMA's masterplan, municipal policy plans and the existing city core, DS landschapsarchitekten has worked out a complete scenario for the public realm. It provides guidelines for organizing the public realm and formulates principles (coherence, embedding and change) for the basic elements, each of which has its own instructions for use and area of application. For example, the floor (paving) of the pedestrian domain is seen literally as the basis for the design of the public realm, trees are used as a means of enticing natural surroundings into the city, water is used as an ordering element, lighting and distinctive features are used to endow a space with meaning and atmosphere.

'Le nouveau jour' Office building

architect: A+D+P Architecten
client: Eurocommerce
construction: from 1999

'Le nouveau jour' office building by A+D+P Architecten takes its inspiration from the discrepancies between the 20 year-old zoning plan and the urbanist ambitions of the OMA masterplan.

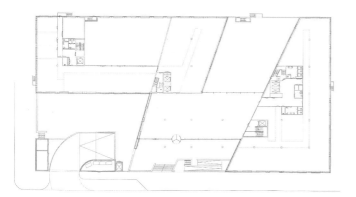

'De Vlinder' Office building

architect: Brouwer Steketee Architecten
client: Nelis Project Maatschappij
construction: from 1999

'De Vlinder' (the butterfly) office building by Brouwer Steketee Architecten, orientates itself in relation to the station and the park. The economically and compactly designed building runs to seven floors and lends itself to a flexible office layout.

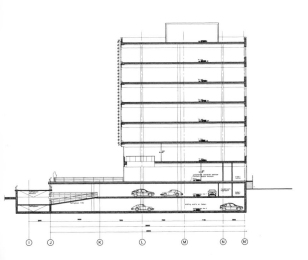

ICT businesses and the 'Alnovum' Institute

architect: Benthem Crouwel Architekten
client: Almere City
construction: 1999 - 2000

In keeping with the spirit of the masterplan by OMA, Benthem Crouwel Architekten's centre for ICT businesses and the 'Alnovum' Institute for Information Engineering consists of two autonomous volumes each with its own character and appearance. The buildings can be operated either separately or in conjunction.

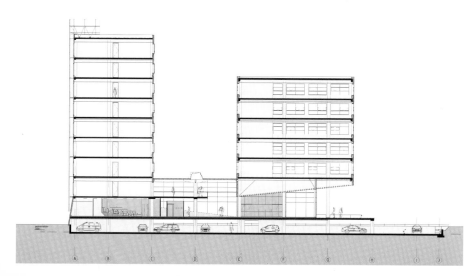

Study for WTC

architect: Urhahn Urban Design
client: Bouwfonds
construction: from 1999

Urhahn Urban Design base their study for the WTC on the masterplan by OMA, commercial criteria and the physical characteristics of the site. OMA's masterplan envisages a compact business centre with a small footprint and striking skyline: a visible quantum leap for Almere. The developers want phased development, efficient access, impressive buildings and a lively environment. The physical characteristics determine the circulation routes, the principal connections and the fact that while the plan seeks to link up with the station concourse it turns its back on the railway lines.

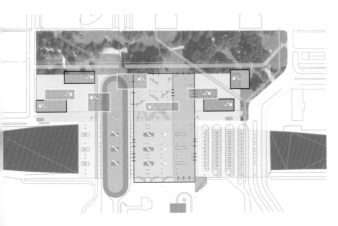

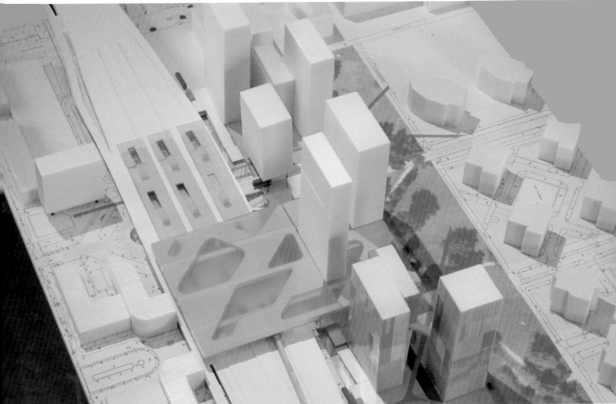

Colophon

Published on the occasion of the exhibition 'Dutchtown', held at the Netherlands Architecture Institute in Rotterdam from 27 November 1999 – 6 February 2000.

design Kitty Molenaar
translation Robyn de Jong-Dalziel (Colenbrander/Provoost, Alkemade); Billy Noland (Feireiss)
Image research Fransje Hooimeijer
lithography and printing SSP Printers
editing/production Barbera van Kooij
publisher Simon Franke

photography
Office for Metropolitan Architecture
Hans Werlemann – cover and all OMA-models
Aerophoto Schiphol b.v., no. 29
Jan Derwig, no. 13, 14
Rob 't Hart, no. 4
Barbera van Kooij, no. 48
Rondo Special Products, Suurland Falkplan b.v., p. 6/7
Ruden Riemens, no. 64
Rijksarchief in Flevoland, fotoarchief nr. zzw-8.715, no. 1
Gert Schutte, no. 11
Sonius Creative Imaging, no. 16
Jan Versnel, no. 6

The exhibition 'Dutchtown' received generous financial support from Ontwikkelingscombinatie Almere Hart CV, the City of Almere and De Weger Architecten- en Ingenieursbureau bv.

Available in North, South and Central America through D.A.P./Distributed Art Publishers Inc, 155 Sixth Avenue 2nd Floor, New York, NY 10013-1507, Tel. 212 627.1999 Fax 212 627.9484

Available in the United Kingdom and Ireland through Art Data, 12 Bell Industrial Estate, 50 Cunnington Street, London W4 5HB, Tel. 181-747 1061 Fax 181-742 2319

Printed and bound in the Netherlands

ISBN 90-5662-140-8